HYPNOSIS WITHOUT WORDS

A PRACTICAL BOOK

DR. SHASHIKANT KALSULKAR

ISBN 979-8-89363-259-0

Just reading the introduction of this book, you are able to *hypnotise* others. After you have finished the reading book, you will be a nonverbal *Hypnotherapist.*

–Dr. Shashikant Kalsulkar

Acknowledgement

I am very much thankful to Dr. Marco Paret from Italy for his teaching on Mesmerism, Magnetism, Fascination and Nonverbal Hypnosis as a Gynaecologist and Obstetrician specialist for more than 40 years. I was working with women and their emotions all the time. I have always felt that there is much more than body and mind. I have always looked for a thread between body, mind, and soul, which is universal energy. I was hungry to learn about energy treatment. I felt there must be more than consulting and treating the patient. I am looking for an opportunity. My journey started with clinical hypnosis in Vienna by Dr Allan Krupka. Of course, I will reach out to Dr. Paret in Rome next. Today, he is the authority figure in nonverbal hypnosis in Europe and perhaps in the world. I also received teachings from Friedbert Becker from Germany, Master Dodie, and Robert Steven from Indonesia. I am most grateful to all of them. In this practical book on nonverbal Hypnosis, you will see their methods .Which I learn from them.

I also thank Antonius Schroer, my friend and colleague on this journey.

I can not end without thanking my son Nicholas, who has helped in the digital and technical side of book writing and my beloved wife who has encouraged and helped me to finish this book.

Preface

I am writing this book for you because I know you are interested in learning more about hypnosis. You want to experience the hypnotic trance. You want to experience your inner self, tap into your imagination power, a dream state. You want to go into daydreaming, you want to be in your "safe place" where you feel free, fresh, relaxed, comfortable, energized, and you want to activate your inner healer. Everybody has the power to activate his or her own inner healer. Your inner healer wants to help not only you but also others. That is an intrinsic quality one has to be born with. Others have to develop it. You are one of them. In that case, you help others to activate their own healing power in a very short time without much communication, silently. It is simple to learn nonverbal hypnosis without words. It looks like magic. The client goes into a trance himself with his own desire and will. We just have to be in the present and in alignment with him all the time between the Universe and Earth like a channel or the medium. Just go through a couple of times reading this practical exercise book, and you can start healing yourself and helping others.

Index

1. **Introduction**...11

Hypnosis Without Words - Nonverbal Hypnosis 11

2. **What is the Nonverbal Hypnosis?**......................14

The Focus is directed inward in Hypnosis....................15

The Electromagnetic waves in the Brain.....................16

3. **How Does Nonverbal Hypnosis Work?** 21

Nonverbal Communication: 21

Nonverbal Hypnosis Tools and Techniques: 22

Hypnotic Points - Areas: 22

Body-Mind and Soul Relation in Hypnosis.................29

4. **Become A Great Nonverbal Hypnotist** 30

Magnetic Eyes - Magnetic Gaze: 30

Magnetic Handshake: 31

Magnetic Breathing...32

Personal Magnetism:..34

Exercise for Presence...35

Exercise of Awareness of Body and Mind: 36

5. **Pre-Talk With Your Client** 38

What is the problem we need to work on? 39

Suggestibility Test: 40

Sensitivity Test: 41

Polarity Test: 41

6. Nonverbal Hypnosis Induction 43

Mesmeric Passes, Touches, and Strokes: 44

Magnetism: 45

Fascination: 47

Head Rotation - Trabona Method: 48

Thump Holding - Lafonte Method: 49

Pushing down The Hands: 49

Oculomotor Blockage: 49

Jellyfish Induction: 50

Gypsy Induction 51

7. Deepening of Trance 52

Relaxation: 52

Catalepsy 53

How do you know that your client is in Somnambulism? .. 56

Regression of Past Event 58

How do you know that your client is in the Ecstasy state?. 63

8. Nonverbal Hypnotherapy 65

Body Pain 67

Headache 67

Backache and Other Muscle and Joint Pain 68

Exercise at Home: 71

Di Pisa's Instant Healing Method:....................... 71

Variation of Treatment Using NLP Technique.................... 74

Negative Emotions of Past Event 75

Variation of Treatment........................ 77

Ball of light 81

Magnetic Massage 82

Magnetic Massage 85

Addictions 85

Weight Loss 91

Exercise to Do at Home 94

9. **Miscellaneous** 95

Self-Hypnosis:........................ 95

Clairvoyance: 97

Telepathy 99

10. **The END** 101

Dehypnosis: 101

Post-hypnotic Suggestions:........................ 102

I call it combo-hypnosis. 103

1

Introduction

Hypnosis Without Words - Nonverbal Hypnosis

My friends ask me, how is Hypnosis without words possible? I tell them, yes, It is not only possible but also easy to learn. You try the Self-Hypnosis and realize that it works. Then, use it on others to help them to solve their problems.

Last week, I was sitting with some friends in a garden Restaurant. I got introduced to a lady school teacher. She asked me what I do for a living . She means my profession. I told her that I am a medical doctor, Gynaecologist but now I am semi-retired and practice nonverbal Hypnosis as it is my hobby and passion. I always felt there is something more than mind- body medicine. I could see that she was surprised and, at the same time, curious. She could not believe me and asked me. How is it possible, doc? She was tall and had a normal build for her age. She had long brown hair. She was sitting opposite me in a comfortable rattan chair. I asked her if she wants to experience hypnotic trance right now. She laughed and said yes.

I got up immediately from my chair and bent forward towards her. I took her right hand in my left hand, holding gently at her right wrist with my left thumb and left middle finger and started elevating it.

At the same time, I showed her with my right hand and pointed to her to concentrate, seeing in my right eye. I focused my eyes between her eyebrows (at the level third eye). I started matching my breathing with her breathing for some time . Then, I started breathing deeply. She followed me with deep breathing. Her eyes were blinking and it was very difficult for her to keep them open. She was in a hypnotic trance. I closed both of her eyes with my right hand. I held her left hand gently with my right hand .It was floppy and relaxed. I raised her hand above her head and pressed the palm of left hand on the crown of her head. I then pressed her left shoulder and forearm,followed by elbow and arm to make them stiff so that they could stay in that position. Now I took her right arm with both of my hands and made it straight above her head and again little pressure on forearm, elbow and arm. Her right hand was also stiff and at shoulder level. That is called a Catalepsy of arms.

Next, I rotated her head 3 or 4 times left to right and then left. Followed by moving both my hands from her head to her abdomen, about 3-5 cm from the body without touching her (It is called mesmeric passes).

Followed by massaging at the level of the navel with circular movements of my right hand without touching her. I told her husband to take her photo with a stiff right hand hanging at the level of her right shoulder.

Then I put her hand slowly, brought it down, and kept hanging it on her right side. I did the same thing to her left hand to hang on the left side of her. Now, she was in deep relaxation for about half an hour.

We decided to wake her up. To wake her up I did some reverse passes without touching her from her navel to her face until eyes and then blowing on her face slowly and touching her face lightly to wake her up. There was a smile on her face.

She felt relaxed, energetic, and peaceful. She has now experienced hypnotic trance. It is possible to go into trance, asleep without using a word .

That is the nonverbal Hypnosis. It is that easy. You can try on your friends too. I used Magnetism, Mesmerism ,Fascination and nonverbal hypnosis methods on her.

If you want to learn this to do on yourself and on others, then go ahead to the next chapter second to know more about nonverbal Hypnosis.

> **Whatever you communicate with words, you are conveying your true beliefs on nonverbal level.**
>
> **–Friedbert Becker**

2

What is the Nonverbal Hypnosis?

The word "Hypnosis" comes from "Hypno," which means sleep, and "osis," which means condition or state. So, hypnosis is a sleep-like condition, although you are not in deep sleep.

Normally, in the waking state, the attention of our mind and body is directed outwards. In deep sleep, our mind and body are resting, with only our vital organs and systems like breathing, circulation, digestion, and glands working in a reduced state to keep us alive.

Now, the third state is when you are neither in deep sleep nor fully awake; this state is called the dreaming state. We go to this stage everyday . When you go to sleep by lying down and closing your eyes on the bed at night before sleep or in the early morning when you are awake but still sleepy and reluctant to get up from the bed, it is called Lucid Sleep (Transparent Sleep) or daydreaming.

This state is also called the Trance State, during which all your senses are working, including hearing, touching, smelling, and even seeing if your eyes are open, but all these outer stimuli do not disturb you at all. Your focus is directed inward. Your intelligent, analytical, logical, conscious mind rests, and you focus on your dreams, imagination, and your own personal world of fantasies in your subconscious mind through the Critical Factor. The Critical Factor acts as a doorkeeper at the gate between your conscious and subconscious mind, allowing only important thoughts for our survival to enter your subconscious mind out of nearly 60,000 thoughts per day.

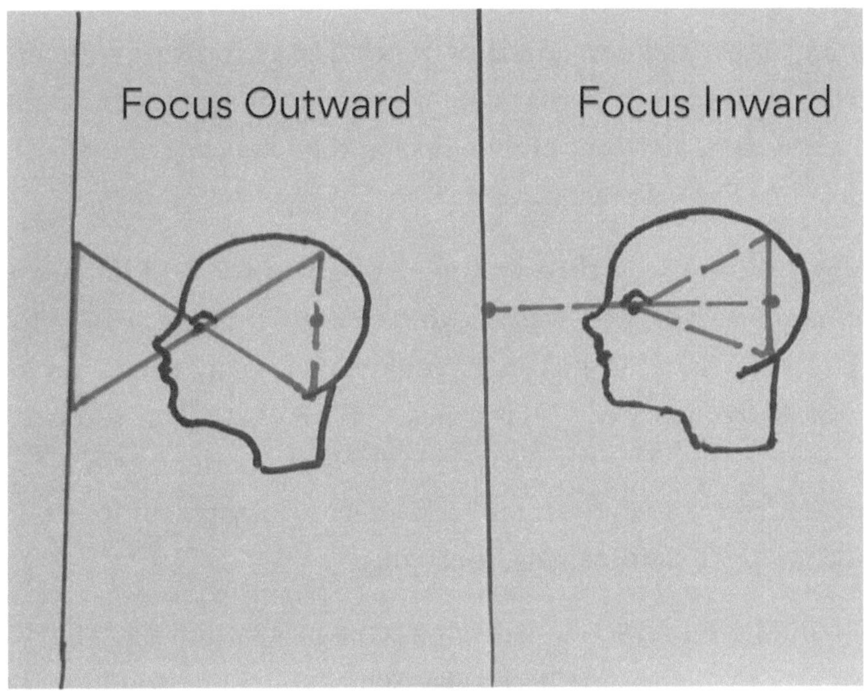

The Focus is directed inward in Hypnosis

The process of going into lucid Sleep or Daydreaming is called Hypnosis. This state of Mind and Body is called the Trance State.

Our brain cells are working through passing electric current in wave form. In the waking state, our brain is very active and works with very high-frequency waves of 16-30 Hz. That is call **BETA waves.**

In the state of deep sleep, our brain works only the minimum necessary and with a very low frequency of 01.to 0.3Hz. That is called **DELTA waves.**

After a whole day of working, when you come home, you just want to rest and hear music or watch TV, even take a bath and relax in your chair. In that state, your Analytical Brain and Body want to rest, and your brain works at the frequency of 8-15 Hz, called **ALPHA Waves.**

Now you are very tired and need to go to bed and lie down, close your eyes, and wait to go to sleep. That stage is called the Dream state. In this state, your brain activity shows a very reduced frequency of 4-7 Hz called **THETA Wave.** You also often experience this Theta wave state in the early morning before you get up, and your eyes are still closed. You do not want to get up and you may start imaging, dreaming.

So, during the hypnotic induction, you go first into the ALPHA state or the light state of Trance. When you allow still more to relax and let go of yourself

The Electromagnetic waves in the Brain

Our brain and spinal cord belong to the central nervous system (CNS). The spinal canal carries messages from the body back and forth through the peripheral nervous system. The autonomic nervous system operates internal organs, smooth muscles, and glands. It regulates daily heart rate, digestion, respiratory rate, pupillary response, urination, and sexual arousal. The brain controls our thinking, learning, movements, feelings, and emotions.

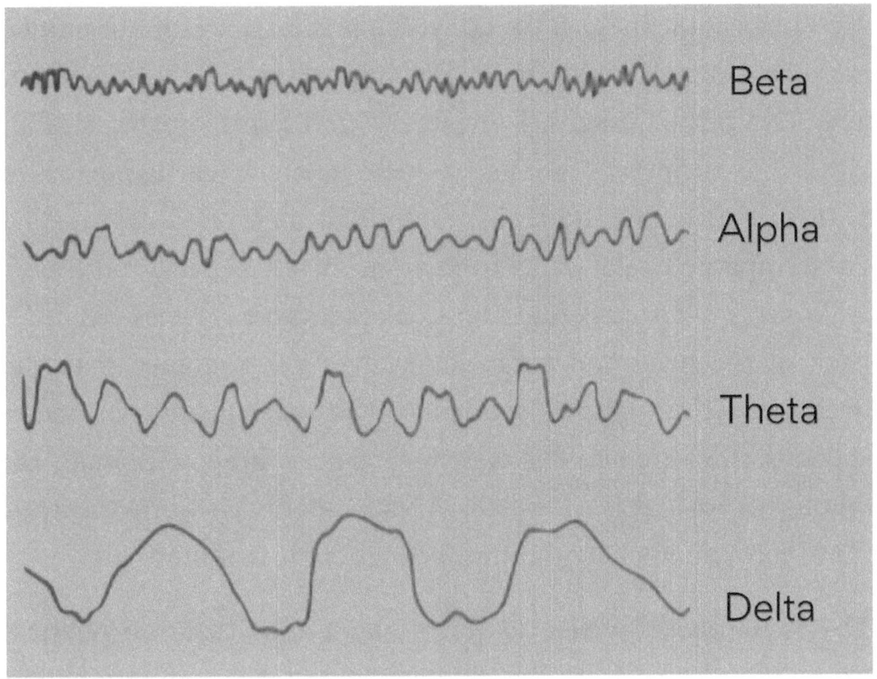

We do not yet know where consciousness is situated in our brain. Scientists have found through electroencephalogram and functional magnetic resonance imaging that our brain has different areas for intelligence, emotions, memory, vision, and other sense organs, but they do not know how they all work together. Who brings all this information together in a synchronized way and acts rightly for our survival and wellness? That is our consciousness. Scientists say that it is the hard problem of consciousness. They do not know that the soul or spirit, the God particle, works through our consciousness and body. Even quantum theory suggests it is all vibrations, waves, and energy—even the Universe... God. When we die, our breath and soul, spirit, go away, leaving our dead body and inactive brain. The air we breathe carries this energy of life... life force.

Now, let's come back to the body. We'll talk about the autonomic nervous system (ANS). It is very important for the hypnotist. The ANS has 2 systems, Sympathetic and Parasympathetic, that work in a reciprocal manner to keep us alive. The sympathetic part primarily manifests in control of fight and flight. The parasympathetic allows us to rest and digest or feed and breed. ANS nerves, through the Vagus, a cranial nerve, pass from the back of the head and chest and end in the abdomen over the intestine, viscera, and solar plexus. This solar plexus is recently called the Enteric nervous system or Enteric brain. Although the whole nervous system—CNS, ANS, and ENS—work together. Now you know where our gut feelings come from.

The sympathetic system is active and aroused during physical stress; blood flow from the gut goes to muscles, respiration, and the brain. The heart rate increases, skin blood vessels constrict, and pupils dilate. It is also responsible for sexual orgasm. The parasympathetic system calms us down for our psychological balance and survival. It is important for relaxation, sleep, meditation, hypnosis, massage, gentle touch, deep contact with another person, and nurturing. We use this system in hypnotic trance deepening for relaxation and letting go. The blood flow increases in the gastrointestinal tract for digestion decreases heart rate, and constricts pupils. It is also important for sexual arousal.

Working throughout the day in and day out, our sympathetic system can not cope with it with its fight and flight response and go in to shut down. We feel burnt out. It is the Dorsal Vagal shutdown. It is a potential physical response to switch to the parasympathetic system. It remains active and the person goes into a state of freeze.

He isolates socially, has no appetite, has slow breathing, low blood pressure and a respiration rate. Sometimes, dizzy and fainting spells. Some call it Polyvagal Syndrome (PVS). We will talk more about PVS in the Nonverbal Hypnotherapy chapter.

Now we go back to Hypnosis and its origin.

Since stone age man knew about dreaming and daydreaming. That time there was no language, only nonverbal gestures and loud sounds. All ancient cultures in all the continents like Indians, Chinese, Egyptians, Greeks and South American tribes knew how to induce the Trance. They then used singing, dancing, drums, Mantras, Loud noise without using words and also projecting life energy like Chi, Prana, Kundalini, Hara on the Subjects.

Although the word "Hypnosis" was invented by Dr. James Braid (1795-1860), a Scottish surgeon, the father of Hypnosis is said to be an Austrian physician, Dr. Franz Anton Mesmer (1734-1815). He believed that there is some kind of fluid or magnetic waves between 2 people, animals, and trees. He called it Magnetism. He started using passes from head to toe of the client, stroking shoulders, and touching different points of the body for about 15-20 minutes to induce a Trance State in his client. He is definitely the father of Nonverbal Hypnosis and Mesmerism. He had a lot of problems with his methods being accepted in medical societies. He had to go away from Vienna to Paris.

There were also physicians who did not accept him. They declare it is a hocus pocus charlatan.

Later, verbal suggestions were introduced by Abbe Faria, an Ind-Portuguese priest who lived in France at the beginning of the 18th century. Slowly speaking was introduced in the induction of hypnosis and verbal hypnosis. This method was accepted in medical Universities. Milton Erickson (1901-1980), a USA Psychiatrist, has brought today's Modern Hypnosis. He is considered to be the father of Modern Hypnosis. It takes a long time to induce a hypnotic trance state in the client in verbal hypnosis. The hypnotist has to talk for most of the session. So now you know what hypnosis is without words and the difference between nonverbal and verbal hypnosis.

In recent years, hypnotherapists have used both in their hypnotherapy use nonverbal and verbal methods to make induction, deepening and therapy fast, easier and more effective.

I call it Combo-Hypnosis like combo meals in fast food restaurants. The hypnotist starts with a non verbal Induction. During deepening trance,therapy and post hypnotic suggestion used language.

> The Secret of Hypnosis is that it takes you to the Unconsciousness and you can put the seed of anything in the Unconsciousness and it will come to blossom, the blossoming happens in the Consciousness but roots remain in the Unconsciousness
>
> –OSHO

3

How Does Nonverbal Hypnosis Work?

The nonverbal hypnosis begins as you see the client. Once you have eye contact with him. Nonverbal communication starts with smiling, curiosity, fascination and attraction.

you can start observing his gestures, facial expressions, body language, vocal tone, and rhythm. If possible, observe his emotions, feelings, and breathing pattern. Studies show that in communication, 55% depends on body language, 38% on tone of voice, and only 7% on content.

Nonverbal Communication:

You start by copying the client's movements of his hands, body, and breathing. If he is moving his hands and body, then take the same steps, mirroring him. That is called pacing. You feel now that he is trusting you and you are synchronized with his body movements and breathing; then, you can change your breathing pattern, and he will follow you. That is called leading. You have built rapport with your client. You can then talk about his problem or agenda without details, which he wants to work on. Otherwise, he can tell us about his negative emotions only if he does not expose his problem.

Nonverbal Hypnosis Tools and Techniques:

We have the following tools: Physical, Sensory organs, Mental, Emotional, and Energy. We will now talk about how the techniques use these tools.

1. **Physical:**

    A) **Breathing:** Synchronizing the breathing with the client and then making him breathe with your tempo. You can use deep hypnotic breathing along with other methods described below.

    B) **Body Movements:** As I mentioned earlier, pacing and leading with the handshake and making posture with the client.

After the handshake and pre-talk, getting closer to the patient, you start touching his right shoulder and ask for permission to touch him.

Hypnotic Points - Areas:

During induction, you start gently touching hypnotic areas or points like in acupuncture points. These are on the head, forehead, back of the neck, chest, sternum, upper back, between the scapula, upper abdomen, shoulders, elbows, hips, knees, and ankles. Sometimes during deepening of hypnotic trance also inducing crisis, you may have to press a little harder on the upper abdomen - in the solar plexus. You will see this in my drawings on the next pages.

During the induction of the trance, go very near to the client in his aura and again go back a meter distance in all directions, making him feel your presence without speaking a word. The long passes from head to toe from front, back, and right and left sides. The client eventually gets confused. During the therapy, you have to guide him with your hand and show him directions to follow you while putting him on the floor.

To make him stiff, cataleptic, and relaxed, since there is no talking, you have to use your hands and the power of your eyes. Since the eye is a sense organ, we will now talk about sense organs.

Hypnotic Points and Areas on the front and back of the Body

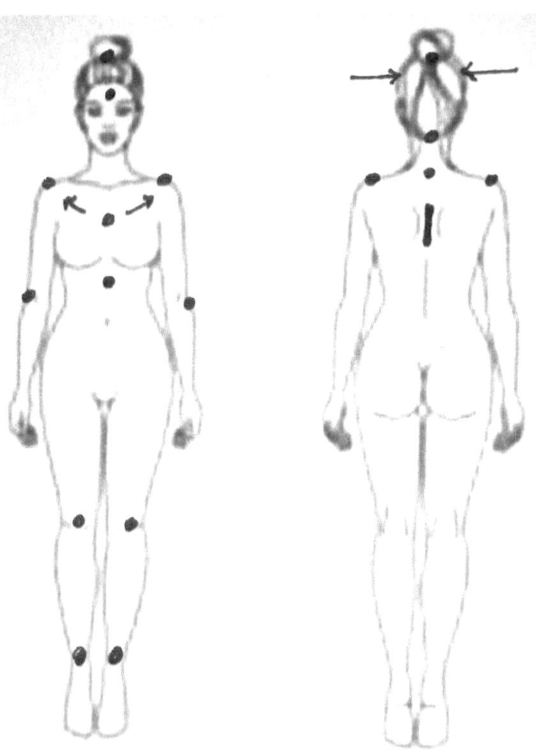

C) **Sense Organs Stimulation:**

i) **Tactile Stimulus:** along with passes, also strokes, random touches, stimulating hypnotic points, or even some acupuncture points, especially using both hands.

ii) **Visual Stimulus – Gaze:** We cannot deny the power of a strong gaze. One can use their attractive charm in induction. Ask the client to look at your right eye nonverbally, pointing with your right hand index finger to your right eye. You look at the client's left eye for a minute or so and then his right eye, which makes him uneasy, and he starts blinking his eyes. You can also stare at his forehead in the region of the third eye. The client's pulse and blood pressure go down. His breathing slows down. His pupil dilates. In the case of gazing into the opposite-sex partner, it increases sexual attraction and arousal. The observer influences the observed.

Through the eye, one expresses sorrow, joy, anger, displeasure, and cheerfulness.

iii) **Auditory Stimulus:** You can give stimulus to his hearing sense. You can hum the mantras like OM as AUM, uttering meaningless sounds... anh...anh..anh... continuously to overload his hearing sense. One can also use music with 3.5- 7.5 Hz stimulating THETA waves

iv) **Sense of Smell and Taste:** Using Incense sticks in the therapy room. The taste stimulation is often not used, only when taste sensations are involved in hypnotherapy. In cases of addictions like smoking to get rid of the taste of the cigarette or in cases of likes and dislikes of food.

Our senses collect information about the outer world and send it to the brain (CNS) through sensory and sympathetic nerves via Cerebrospinal nerves.

Our subconscious mind is responsible for 95% of our brain processing only 5% for our conscious and critical factors. The conscious mind has only 5% capacity to use for analytic and logical thinking, willpower, short memory, and critical factors. The critical factor is the part of the Limbic brain that works day and night to keep us safe. Did you know that in our awake state during the day, like working, talking, planning, creating, etc., we only access 5% of our brain? Our subconscious mind is like an automatic machine running in the background, working day and night, using 95% of our brain capacity to keep us alive. It deals with our long-term memory, beliefs, emotions, fears, values, intuition, imagination, self-image, dreams, and fantasies. It is protecting us by controlling all the systems in the body.

In short, we cannot access our subconscious mind when our conscious mind is at work in the waking state. So, in order to get into the subconscious mind, we have to find a way to get into our subconscious mind without knowing the gatekeeper - the critical factor. Only then will we be able to arrive at the THETA waves state from the ALPHA Waves state in our brain?

Hypnosis is one of the ways to bypass critical factors to access our subconscious mind. In self-hypnosis, you have to manage yourself. In the case of induction through a hypnotist, they guide you to achieve this theta wave state.

2. **Mental:**

   a) **Intention:** Your desire, will, and intention to help the client. You can start visualizing a mental picture or a film of what you desire your client to do. Then, with your strong will, you project that image onto the client.

   b) **Nonverbal Suggestions:** Usually, we use quite a lot of nonverbal suggestions in our daily life without even realizing. In school, teachers tell children to sit down, stand up, come forward, or go back with hand gestures. We often use our hands and fingers to instruct others without words. We use nonverbal suggestions with clients in hypnotherapy.

Examples: Ask the client to focus their eyes on your right eye by showing with your right hand finger. If you want your client, standing, to fall backward, you go to their back and touch their shoulders from behind, slowly pulling back without any words.

3. **Emotions:**

   i) **Identify:** Look at the client to notice their emotional state. They may be nervous about hypnosis if it is their first experience. You make them comfortable through pacing, leading, and rapport.

ii) **Empathy and Sympathy:** Try to feel their emotions. In the pre-talk with your client, they may tell you where they feel their emotions in their body. Concentrate your gaze in that area.

iii) **Change the emotional state:** Try to change their negative emotions, if any, during the hypnotherapy into a positive emotional state.

4. Energy:

Since ancient cultures, humans have known about the existence of universal sun energy and Mother Earth's magnetic energy. It is believed that both energies meet in living beings at the center and form life energy. Chinese call it Chi or Qi. Indians call it Prana. Dr Anton Franz Mesmer called it Earth magnetic energy.

All the material in this universe is in the form of energy waves. We are already aware of light, electric, and magnetic energies.

Especially now, with the development of TVs, phones, mobiles, and computers, such energies exist. Through the knowledge of quantum theory, one can explain energy presence very well. All solid matter is formed of tiny atoms. These atoms are formed by electromagnetic waves. We cannot see these waves, but we can feel them. The human body is made up of tiny cells, which are also made up of atoms, hence electromagnetic waves. Even our thoughts and emotions are all forms of energy. If we stay in our negative emotions and thoughts, we will lose our energy. In sickness, we realize we are very weak and have less power to do normal things.

When we compare our being to a motor car, our body is like the chassis, our mind is like the engine, and you yourself sit in the driving seat. Without diesel, petrol, and now in electric cars, electricity, your car will not run at all. Here, obviously, "you" means your soul.

So that is how we can see the connection between body, mind, energy, and soul. All living beings have a small particle of the Universe, the Creator or God, called a God particle - soul, spirit. The soul, through our mind and body, lives our life. The soul is always happy, joyful, peaceful, and blissful. When we are born as babies, we know only these emotions since our minds have no memory of their own by birth. As the child grows, it collects memories from its environment, parents, and teachers. With these memories, emotions are stored. Often, negative emotional stories are stored, though some positive emotions are also stored. There might be some memories from past lives, but the child does not remember them anymore once their own experiences and memories are stored in their brain.

We keep reacting to the world around us, using our stored memories with emotions, mostly negative, though, of course, there are some positive ones, too. In this mind and body circuit, we react to stimuli based on how we have learned to react in the past.

> **The Memory can exit without Imagination but Imagination can not exit without Memory.**
>
> —Abbe Faria

Body-Mind and Soul Relation in Hypnosis

Most of the time, we all forget that we are blissful beings. We are God particles; we have all the Golden Buddha within us. Once you know that, life will be simple, without conflict, and full of peace, joy, and bliss. In a hypnotic trance, you may delve into this bliss Ecstasy and get to know your true self. In hypnosis, you can reach a state of bliss that features characteristics of your soul. Although it is transient, you experience and know that you are a blissful being in your true nature.

Hypnotherapy works with all these elements possible. A Nonverbal hypnotist can train themselves to initiate, store, and use this energy during their treatment sessions.

Now, we will go to the next chapter to learn how to train to access this energy.

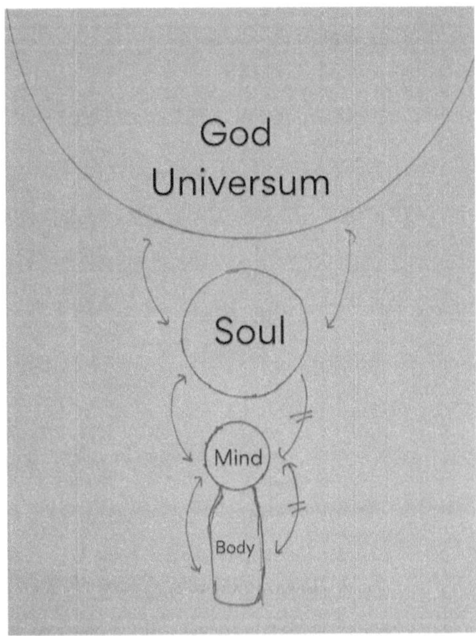

4

Become A Great Nonverbal Hypnotist

To become a successful nonverbal hypnotist, you also have to train yourself to stay present, here and now. If you're busy with your own problems from the past or anxious about the future, you cannot help others. You have to be a magnetic person. I will explain later in this chapter how to be magnetic in front of your clients and provide exercises to develop your personal Magnetism. To increase your personal Magnetism, you have to train your gaze and breathing and initiate, store, and use electromagnetic energy through your thoughts, emotions, and hands. You should learn the art of intelligent listening, earnestness in talking, develop strong willpower, and physical and moral fearlessness.

Magnetic Eyes - Magnetic Gaze:

I have already discussed how "the observer influences the observed." With the gaze, you try to hold the attention of the person. We train our eyes so we can transmit our intention and willpower to others. That is the law of mental control. You develop a strong gaze that can manifest fear in others for a few seconds. With your fixed, interesting, sweetly penetrating, expressive eyes on your client, they will be fascinated and soon go into hypnotic trance. Now, you have to exercise daily for at least 6 weeks, preferably 6 months, to gain this magnetic power in your eyes.

i) **Mirror Exercise:** You can mark a black point on the mirror and stand in front of it about 30 cm away, staring at the dark point daily. Start with 5 minutes and slowly increase up to 15-20 minutes. You can also stare at your right eye, then left eye, the root of the nose, or at the level of the third eye on your forehead instead of marking a black point.

ii) **Cardboard Exercise:** Prepare a black cardboard disc with a white spot in the center. Hang the disc on the wall and fix your gaze on the white spot. Move your head around the circle.

iii) **Circular Influence:** Sit in a chair looking at the wall in front of you and look right, left, up, and down in circles to increase your peripheral vision.

The eye possesses the power to act as a reservoir of energy as well as a transmitter of energy.

Magnetic Handshake:

When you are shaking the hand of your client or, in general, shaking hands to introduce yourself, always bend slightly towards the person and look at the root of his nose without blinking and thinking what you wish him to do. Then, he grasps his hand firmly but not so hard as to cause pain. Take hold of as much of the hand as possible; never take hold of fingers so quickly that he can close his fingers and prevent you from grasping his full hand. Then, shake his hand up and down once only. Hold his hand for a few seconds. As you are withdrawing your hand away, let your fingers slide over his fingers.

You start training yourself with every hand shake and you will be surprised at how it is so easy to influence others.

Magnetic Breathing

There are various breathing techniques to increase, store, and utilize your energy, not only for influencing others but also for your own health and charisma.

In Pranayama, an Indian breathing technique, there are many methods for enhancing health and spirituality.

Basically, you have to breathe through your nose, hold your breath, and exhale slowly and steadily through the nose to store energy in the body and to release the energy through the slightly open mouth towards the client. There are various methods to train your breathing. Principle is that you inhale air deep in your belly ,hold it and then exhale slowly through your nose. That is called Deep Abdominal Breathing. If you imagine inhaling Universal energy along with inhalation and during exhalation through nose imaging you store that energy in your stomach, in the solar plexus.

 I will explain 3 methods here, but if you want to learn more, you have to read further about Pranayama.

   i)   **Triangular Breathing:** (7-7-7) During inhalation, count 1..2..3..4..5..6..7 in your mind or aloud. Hold the breath for 7 counts and exhale, also counting 7 times.

   ii)   **Quadrant breathing:** (7-3-7-3) During inhalation, count 7 times, hold for only 1..2..3.   and exhale again 7 times.

The difference here from triangular breathing is that after exhalation again, hold your breath 3 times.

iii) **Alternate nasal breathing:** Using your right hand thumb, close your left nostril and ring finger and pinkie finger, closing your right finger. Start inhalation from the left nostril and close the left nostril with the ring and pinkie finger. Hold your breath, then exhale from the right nostril by holding the left nostril with your thumb. Here, breathing counts are 4-16-8.

Short, deep inhalation, only 4 times, then holding your breath for 16 times and exhaling slowly 8 times.

Tip: If you to relax after heavy hard work, you want to go into ALPHA Wave state. You have to activate the parasympathetic nervous system through breathing only in and out through your left nostril holding the right nostril tight with a ring and little finger for 5 minutes. You will go into physical and mental relaxation.

You can use this short exercise on your client before starting the hypnotic session, and you can also do it with them, so both of you are relaxed. Especially if you notice your client is anxious and nervous about the situation, you can even perform triangular or quadrant breathing.

During exhalation, pull your buttocks (pelvic muscles) in and project the idea onto the client by looking with magnetic eyes at their forehead or stomach (solar plexus). If you are standing behind the client, focus on the back of their neck.

Personal Magnetism:

You have to develop your personal Magnetism through different body exercises and learn to stay in the present. You have to train your visual, auditory, tactile, olfactory, and gustatory sensory modalities, as well as your thought processes and emotions. Here are some exercises -

Exercise to Increase Your Power:

Stand up straight with your legs open slightly and raise both hands with Faust straight above your head.

Take a deep breath and hold it. Then, bend down slowly until your hands are just touching the floor or as far as your hands go down towards the floor.

Still holding their breath, squeezing the buttocks and pressing the chin on the chest. Stay in this position as much as you can, hold your breath, and then slowly raise up your hands above the head, still holding your breath, then slowly bring down your hand to the shoulder and then down the side of your trunk. Now, slowly exhale through your mouth. Do this 3 times.

Exercise to Increase Your Attention:

i) **Point Fixation:** to increase your gaze. Focus your attention on any object in front of you, first a nearby object and then one in the periphery. It can be anything, like a flower plant in front of you and a tree in the distance.

ii) **Finger Fixation:** with your left index finger pointing and other fingers closed, bring it towards the center of the palm of your right hand without touching. Hold it for a few seconds, imagining you are holding a sharp blade. You may feel strong sensations or light pain in your palm.

iii) **Hand Rubbing:** Rub your palms together until you feel tingling sensations and warmth in your palms.

Exercise for Presence

i) **STOP and GO** – to train your sense organs

How do you learn to stay here and now? In this exercise, you train your sense organs. Here, you have to concentrate on one sense organ at a time. For the rest of the sense organs activities, you do not have to take in your Awareness.

Standing straight with legs closed. Arms open straight at the level of the shoulder with your right palm upward and left palm downward second without thought in your mind.

After a few seconds, you start commanding yourself VISUAL– then you concentrate only on seeing what you can see in front of you for a few seconds. All other sensations do not bother you,

Then say GO. Again, stay like that for a few seconds and say STOP. (This can say laud or in your mind.)

AUDITORY- then concentrate on hearing only.

After a few seconds, say End of stop, so with TACTILE-concentrating on our bodily temperature and pressure points, feel the feet on the Earth.

Bring in your Awareness if you feel pain sensations in your body. Feel your Breathing and Heart beats. Followed by OLFACTORY- sensations by thinning of different types of smells around you. With GUSTATORY- if you taste sensation at present or thinking of your tasty food preferences or what you eat last.

You can do this exercise standing, sitting with your hand straight in front of you, or even bending in front of you. It is fun when you do it with friends. You can do with your client to get in your rapport.

ii) **Horse Stand**: In Qigong, this exercise is used for presence and to increase Chi or Qi. Stand straight with knees slightly bent forward, elbows with palms facing upward. Your backbone (sacrum) should align in a straight line with the base of the back of the head (occiput). Feel as if your head is very light and attached to a string hanging from above. Keep your weight on your thighs. Stay in this position for 15 minutes. You can stand in this position for up to 45 minutes.

Exercise of Awareness of Body and Mind:

Similar to meditation, close your eyes and start feeling awareness of your breath. Feel the air going through the air at the tip of your nose, into your lungs, and coming out. Inhale a long, deep breath and exhale slowly. Each time you inhale, concentrate on body parts and organs, feeling them relaxed. Start with your right toes, then left toes, feet, legs, hips, lower back, lower abdomen, upper back, upper abdomen, thorax, neck, face, mouth, nose, eyes, ears, head, forehead, crown, and then the back of the head. At the end of this exercise, you will feel total relaxation.

Variation of This Exercise:

When you feel parts of your body totally relaxed, eventually release and let go. For example, feel your right toe and imagine it in your mental picture. Feel it totally relaxed, release, and let go. At the end of the exercise, you won't feel your body and mind. You'll only feel peaceful, joyful, and blissful. Your inner self, your Golden Buddha. This is called YOGA INDRA.

To become a great nonverbal hypnotist, you have to have a sound body and mind, full of vital energy. Make sure you are smelling nice, wear presentable clothes, and maintain a smile on your face at all times. Learn to stay vertically straight with shoulders slightly forward, feel your feet on the ground, and with a positive mindset; now you are ready to receive your first client.

As your client enters your office, notice their gestures, mimicry, and try to read their emotions. Start pacing and leading to establish rapport. Do not forget to give them a magnetic handshake.

> **We are living in an Ocean of Energy like Fish in the Ocean who do not know that water exist**
>
> **–Dr. Franz Anton Mesmer**

5

Pre-Talk With Your Client

Since our hypnotic induction is without Word, we want to build a rapport as early as possible at the first visit and even on the phone for an appointment. We have to talk to our client before starting the hypnotic induction. We have to ask if he had any experience of hypnotic Trance. You have to explain how Hypnosis works . In a hypnotic induction session, he will feel totally relaxed and sleepy, but still, he can see, hear, feel, Smell and taste. His sense organs are attentive working. He would not do anything that he did not want to do against his beliefs and faith. Tell him, in short, about the conscious mind and subconscious mind and how his subconscious mind helps him and is ready to find a solution for his best. He does not have to disclose his problems in detail in this nonverbal hypnotherapy session, and the solution his subconscious mind will find for him is not given by the therapist. That is the difference between verbal and nonverbal hypnosis. Once, I had a woman in my office for the first time, and we talked about her problem. She told me that she already had some sessions of Hypnotherapy. So, I did not tell her about how hypnosis works and forgot to tell her that the session would be nonverbal. Although people know that I am a nonverbal Hypnotherapist and I work in silence. We had about an hour-long session. At the end, I ask about her experience. She could work on her negative emotions in the Trance and felt strongly working on the solution. Then she said but and stopped for a movement. Tell me more why but ? I said it to her. Then, laughingly, she told me that you did not talk with me during the whole session with a single word. I could see a question mark on her face.

I could not stop laughing. I then told her that I worked nonverbally during the sessions.

Sometimes I use some vocals, mantras and relaxing music. Successively we had then 2 more sessions and she was satisfied with my work.

We talked about magnetic handshakes in the last chapter. You have a chance to feel their fingers. If they are warm, that means they are comfortable and not afraid about hypnosis, especially at the first session. As a gynecologist for 40 years, I have experience with handshakes, especially women's handshakes. You can feel it from the handshake- whether it is warm, cold, trimmer, shy, bossy, or even angry, sad, or fearful- just touching someone's hands. Start practicing from today.

What is the problem we need to work on?

The client does have to tell his whole story, his past life. Of course, if he is eager to tell you. You should listen actively. Otherwise, he can tell you about his problem in short and his feelings and emotions.

Ask him when it started for the first time if he remembers. Where does he feel his emotions in the body? He may have body pain; then ask him the exact area on the body where he feels pain to localize the pain.

You may start by touching him and putting your hand on his back, and touching the hypnotic points. These points are explained in the next chapter. Take the hands slowly away from his back and see if he follows your hand in small movements of his eyes or his body towards you. That is a positive sign. Of course, you have to seek permission before touching him and inform him that you are going to touch different hypnotic points.

Since he does not have to do much, he should just relax, release, and let it go and have a healing experience without talking during the session. It is totally peaceful, tranquil, and meditative.

Before you go for a hypnotic induction in the next chapter, we have to perform suggestibility tests, and sensitivity tests and assess his polarity to our clients to work with him.

Suggestibility Test:

There are many suggestibility tests. You stay behind him and touch his shoulders from behind with your hands, and ask him to fall back. Here, your intention is to produce a mental image in your mind as he is falling backward and project this image onto him with your strong willpower, saying to yourself in your mind, "Do it — do it." Now, without touching his shoulders but still in his aura, if he falls back, he is suggestible. You can try again with more distance between his back and your hands. You may have to massage his shoulders beforehand to gain his trust, especially with difficult clients. You can try the same to make him fall forward.

Sensitivity Test:

This test is done to find out his sensitivity reactions to the magnetic energy field. You should start doing passes in very slow motion in front of him from the top of his head down up to his abdomen- solar plexus. Then, with both hands, sides of the head up to shoulder again and again with a magnetic gaze. Then, slowly try to bring your hands from the crown to his ears, and then try to move your hands forward slowly. Sometimes, you go with your face backwards, suggesting to him nonverbally to come forward as in a suggestibility test. Your intention-mental image,-your Willpower- projecting on him- thinking he is doing it. Try many times if it comes forward and goes backwards with your face.

Polarity Test:

Ask the client to close his hands with fingers interlocking. If his left thumb is on top of the right thumb, he has a creative, artistic nature and works from the right hemisphere of his brain. That is called feminine polarity. He is more sensitive on his left side. They are easy persons to put into the hypnotic trance. The majority of women are like this, which is why we see women easily going into trance.

If you look at his right thumb on top and his left thumb under the right one, then you can conclude that he is a logical, analytical thinker with strong willpower. That is masculine polarity, and the left hemisphere of the brain is more active. He may be difficult to induce into a hypnotic trance and may take a long time to relax and enter a trance. He may need slow induction methods, which you will discuss in the next chapter.

> **The Observer influences the reality he is Observing.**
>
> –Warner Heisenberg

6

Nonverbal Hypnosis Induction

There are various methods of Induction of Hypnotic Trance nonverbally. Even when you are doing Self-Hypnosis on yourself, you have to induce a Trance first. The point of fixation or gaze is using steadily looking at the light (even light from your mobile phone will do), candle, crystal ball, a glass of water preferably crystal glass, a pendulum, looking at the finger or palm of the hand, looking at your own eyes in the mirror. At the same time, ask him to concentrate on his breathing if he has an emotion to work on. He should feel it in his body. Breathing, Gazing and concentrating on his feelings and emotions at the same time.

Give him 2 or more tasks and explain him in Pre-talk so that he knows what to do beforehand. Since our induction and treatment are nonverbal, Sometimes Hypnotists use hamming mantras or utter some sounds like...ahn..ahn..ahn... etc.

We are going to learn some of the techniques- Mesmerism, Magnetism, Fascination, Head Rotation, Thumb holding, Pushing down hands, Oculomotor, Gypsy, Jellyfish etc. Depending on your client, one can use a combination of these methods.

There are three principles of hypnotic Induction.

1) **Shock principle** - you make a surprise movement before the client ot it,

Example-You stretch your right hand forward to shake the client's hand. As he puts his right hand forward,you pull it down at the same time, hold his neck from back with your right hand and bend him towards you.He will not have even time to think what is happening.

2) **Breaking the Pattern principle** - You break the pattern of the task which you have asked the client to perform. Example - **Pushing down hands**- see details in this chapter Induction no.6.

3) **Fatigue or Overload principle**- You give 3 or more tasks at the same time. Example- The client has to breathe deeply along with hand movements at the same time focus on light and concentrate on the solar plexus. He will get tired and close his eyes.

Mesmeric Passes, Touches, and Strokes:

Ask your client to stand in front of you, sit in a chair, lie down on the bed and concentrate on a light or an object in front of him, or even close his eyes using your right hand finger. Tell him not to think and concentrate on his bodily feelings and perceptions.

Then, you also concentrate on what you are going to do. Rub both palms of your hands to energize them, and with the intention of putting your client into a hypnotic sleep or trance, visualize the image in front of you and project it onto him with your willpower. Balance his head by touching his forehead and the back of his head.

Now, stay in front of the client. If he is standing, bring both hands on the top of his head with palms facing his head's top and start bringing them down slowly - right hand on the right side of his head and neck and left hand on the left side of his head and neck about 5 cm from the skin without touching him. Once you touch his shoulders, stroke them on both sides and bring them down to his elbows till his hands, then take your touching fingers away. Ensure that the palms of your hands are facing outwards and upwards, away from the client, making a circle-like motion, and slowly bring them up again to the top of his head.

Then with the right hand in front of the client's head and the left hand behind, start bringing them down slowly over the head, face, neck, then chest, abdomen, especially at the solar plexus in front with the right hand and at the back - head, neck, spine, slowly sliding down with the left hand.

Follow by touching the upper abdomen at the solar plexus level. You can even perform clockwise rotations of your right hand and the left hand at the back at the same level. Then, continue doing such pass strokes in front, back, and sides for at least 15-20 minutes. Normally, in practice, you may take only 5 minutes, and your client goes into a hypnotic trance. Then, proceed to the next stage, fractionation and deepening of trance. You can also perform these passes in a sitting position. In a lying position, you may only need to do them in front.

Magnetism:

To perform magnetic induction, the client should stand in front of you with his feet close together and his head tilted slightly upward, focusing his eyes on the light or any object in front of him, and ask him not to blink his eyes. When he cannot keep them open anymore, then he can close them.

At the same time, he has to concentrate on his upper abdomen, solar plexus, and his breathing - inhalation and exhalation. If he has an emotion, he should bring it to the solar plexus and visualize his emotion at the solar plexus. You stand on the right side of your client. Start by synchronizing your breathing with the client's breathing. Slowly take a few steps away from the client, making a slight noise with your shoes with each step so that he hears and looks for it in his mind. Randomly move slowly front and back, to the sides, go near to him, and then go away a meter or so with shoe steps and come again. During this, you utter some sounds like "ahn..ahn..ahn..."

Start deep breathing, deep inhalation, and deep exhalation. Make him also breathe fast and heavily, deeply breathing with you. All of this should be done nonverbally, showing your chest and his, and your deep breaths, and moving his hands faster and faster in a front and back direction. When you are going near and far from him, every time you come near him, touch him randomly from the front, back, and sides on different parts of his body.

By concentrating on his eyes and solar plexus, deep breathing, moving his hands faster and faster, your touches, sounds, and your movement around in all directions, he becomes confused and overloaded with your nonverbal suggestions. When his eyes are continuously blinking and about to close, at that moment, go behind him, hold him with your hands between his armpits, and pull his body towards your front, your chest. Slowly lay him down straight on the floor on a mattress or yoga mat. During the fall, he will go into a deep trance. You can then induce stiffening of the hands and legs with your both hands pressing his muscles and joints of arms and legs. That is called catalepsy. The client goes into a further deepening of the trance called Fractionation.

Fascination:

Before starting the induction, tell your client to relax and let go. By touching his shoulders and upper arms, move his hands in forward and backward movements. Stay in front of your client. Put your right hand around his neck and keep firm forward pressure behind his neck.

Ask him to look at your right eye and not to blink. You concentrate looking at his left eye with the intention of putting him to sleep, squeezing your buttocks, and during a long exhalation after deep inhalation, keeping your mouth slightly open, project the picture onto him with your willpower that he will be fascinated and go into a hypnotic sleep. Check again if your client is relaxed and loose at his shoulders and hands. Now, look at his forehead, move your right hand to the left side of the client's face slowly, move forward, and attract him towards you. Simultaneously, move your upper body backward and project your intention with energy and mental image, firmly saying in your mind that your client should move forward towards you. The client may lean or tilt towards you. Think in your mind that he is coming forward. Make sure all this time you have a stupid, naive, curious look on your face. You can stop the procedure by blowing on his face and starting the procedure again. It is called Fractionation. It helps to deepen the Trance. You can do 2-3 times so the client gets confused.

Next, slowly pull up the client's right hand with your left thumb and middle finger holding his right wrist, while at the same time pressing down his hand with your left ring finger. Here, pulling up the hand and pushing down creates still more confusion for the client nonverbally. In Fascination induction, the client normally closes his eyes after blinking often and feels tired, but sometimes his eyes may remain open the whole time during the trance. So, you can close them or he can keep them open. There is no harm.

Head Rotation - Trabona Method:

Tell your client that everybody has a pendulum inside them. If he has a negative emotion to work on during the trance, he should bring it to the solar plexus. Then, ask him to look at the light in front of him and a little above his head so that he has to tilt his head up to look at the light. When his eyes are blinking and tired, he should close them. At the same time, he has to breathe heavily and deeply. Then, hold his head with your right hand on the forehead and your left hand on the back of the head. Next, start clockwise rotations like a pendulum. Eventually, the client does it automatically. You hold the hand about 5 cm away from the head and do not touch his head.

He will go into a trance and keep moving his head all the time. Now you can do some passes in front of him. Put some music on for relaxation.

Thump Holding - Lafonte Method:

This is a simple induction. The client and you both sit on chairs in front of each other, with touching knees. Tell the client to look at your forehead or left eye, and you look at his forehead with the intention that he will soon go into a trance. You hold his right and left thumbs with your left and right thumb. Tell him not to blink. Even if he blinks, it does not matter; then he can close his eyes. When he closes his eyes, you start performing mesmeric passes. Go ahead and induce catalepsy of his right and left hand.

Actually, they are already partially cataleptic through thumb holding, since his induction may take 10-15 minutes, but it is enjoyable for the client.

Pushing down The Hands:

It is a similar thumb holding induction. In a sitting position, you hold your hands with palms looking upward, supporting your thighs. Ask the client to put the palms of his hands on your palms, pushing down very hard as much as he can and concentrating on his breathing. At a sneaky moment, pull your right hand away, bring it behind his head, and bend him down. Now, make sure that his hands are hanging beside his thighs. You can then do mesmeric passes on his back.

Oculomotor Blockage:

This is a very simple induction method. One can use it for self-hypnosis too. The client should look at the top of his head for

30 seconds and then close his eyes. Actually, it is very difficult to keep his eyes open and eventually, he goes into a trance.

Jellyfish Induction:

This induction can be used for bad experiences, psychological pain, and negative stuck emotions since childhood. In this method of induction, you can proceed to past event regression or even past life regressions.

You ask the client to feel his emotion in his body. Then ask him to concentrate on the light or a fixed point in front of him just above the head so he has to tilt his head a little upward. You stand in front of him and open both hands, showing him to do that. Then ask him to breathe deeply with you. During inhalation, bring the hands together on the front of the chest and during exhalation, open the hands as much as possible.

Continue this inhalation with hands bringing inside and exhalation hands pushing outside faster and faster; eventually, his eyes start flickering, and he gets tired and cannot do anymore. Go back to him and put your hands between his Axilla. Then, pull his body onto your chest and slowly put him down. Keep holding his left hand straight up with your left hand and start moving his head right to left and left to right with your right hand. You can then induce catalepsy of the left hand and deepen the trance. You can then go ahead with your hypnotherapy. It is so easy. You need a little practice. You can also use this induction method for therapies like Crisis, Hypnodrama, and Regression of past events or past life regression.

Gypsy Induction

These inductions were used by Gypsies, as the name suggests, to cheat people, falsely telling them to see people's future and steal money and things from them.

It is a quick induction. Take the right hand of the client, facing palm towards him, and ask him to imagine what he wants in the future. Then, ask him to look at your eyes or a light in front of him to focus. Tell him to close his eyes if they are tired. Then start moving his hand in round circles around his face. Alternatively, he can focus at the center of his palm where his imaginary wish is placed and keep rotating. Meanwhile, you can mantra energy by humming... Rim... Rim.. Rim... near his head and ears. When his eyes start blinking often, you can press the same right hand on his forehead or top of his head and hold and press the hand. You also have catalepsy of his right hand. You may push his head forward by pressing at the back of his head. There are many more nonverbal and combo methods of hypnotic induction. I am sure you will learn them as you go in this path of nonverbal hypnosis.

7

Deepening of Trance

You have successfully induced your client. Now go ahead and deepen the hypnotic trance. That is called **Fractionation**. Otherwise, the client will open his eyes immediately at the end of the induction if he is still struggling at the Critical Factor with his conscious mind and may not have access to his subconscious mind. Once you are in his subconscious mind and dealing with his emotions and start working on his problem. Generally, it takes 15-20 minutes. He may then stay peacefully in his lucid Sleep, trance for a few more minutes.

The client goes from the conscious state to the subconscious state through the doorkeeper, the Critical Factor.

This brings the client into the state from BETA to ALPHA state during this stage in relaxation of muscles.

Relaxation:

The state of being free from tension and anxiety. You have to guide your client into this state.

Method

Your aim is to make him deeper and deeper in relaxation by moving the client's head right to left and left to right, touching his crown of the head and forehead, even with a little pressure on the third eye region and thinking in your mind of stimulating his third eye. Followed by long passes from head to toe, until he goes into a deep relaxed state.

Catalepsy

A prolonged muscular rigidity and immobility, in which a person's limbs remain in an unnatural, fixed position. After deep relaxation, you start making your client go into a state of stiffness, rigidity called Catalepsy.

Method

The next step is to hold his right hand straight in front of him or above the shoulder, supporting the elbow and pressing the muscle of the upper arm and arm by giving him nonverbal suggestion to hold his hand straight and stiff. Go ahead and do the same to his left hand or bring his left hand, fixing it on his head again with a little pressure on the muscles.

In case he is unable to keep the hands straight and stiff, then try to move it to the original position and then let them fall beside him, hanging in total relaxation if he is sitting. Next to his thighs if he is lying down. You notice they will be floppy. It does not matter. He is still in a relaxed state. In that case , continue performing mesmeric passes and you may try again.

Once his hands and legs are stiff, and if you are presenting to an audience and you want to show them complete body catalepsy, go ahead and make his hands, legs, back muscles, and neck muscles stiff by pressing and imagining his whole body is cataleptic. Then, you can put him straight in between 2 chairs with the help of 2 strong assistants, like in stage hypnosis you may have seen or in YouTube videos.

How do you know that your client is in the Cataleptic stage?

Here are some nonverbal signs you have to look for:

i.   Closing or flickering in his eyes with wide-open pupils.

ii.   Deep breathing.

iii. Redness in the face, chest, and hands due to increased blood flow in these areas.

iv.   Sweating in the hands and feet.

v.   Hands and legs are first relaxed and, in a later stage, stiff. The stiffness of muscles, catalepsy.

vi.   Blood vessels and veins in the neck area are swollen and full of blood.

vii. Ideomotor movements - involuntary muscle movements of the fingers.

viii. 70% of clients experience this hypnotic stage as Catalepsy, the first hypnotic induction.

The next deeper stage of hypnotic trance is called Somnambulism. It means sleepwalker, one who walks around in sleep. That we see in abrupt or limited arousal from deep non rapid eye movements (Non-REM) sleep . That is a THETA waves state.

The client reaches this stage once he starts working on his problem with its emotions once he is in the Somnambulism state.

The client's hand and legs go into contractual, rapid, involuntary hand and leg movements in all directions. Sometimes crying, loud uttering words or shouting, and even strong fit-like movements of the whole body are called crises. Sometimes, the hypnotherapist may have to help the client reach this stage called Crisis so that he can bring his emotions from the mind into the body, get released, and eventually let go and replace them with positive emotions.

Method:

Your client is already in hypnotic deep relaxation and in the cataleptic stage. If he goes himself into the crisis stage, then you just guide him with your hands. If you see that your client is struggling with signs of crafting, you want to help him to get rid of his bad emotions at this stage. Best to help him go into crisis. The crisis is better to do in a lying position, but it is also possible to do it in sitting and standing.

i. Move his head from side to side.

ii. Stimulate hypnotic points on his chest and heart by tapping on the sternum and upper abdomen by massaging the solar plexus area.

iii. Imagine and visualize the picture of your client performing a crisis in front of you, in your mind projecting on the client with your power and energy with contracting pelvic floor after deep inhalation during exhalation that the client brings his problem from his mind to his body. You may utter some words in his ears and show him how to move his hands and legs with your hands and what he should do, of course nonverbal.

iv. Follow with bending both of his legs at the knee by putting feet together touching each other. With little force, he will then continue moving his legs. The moving the legs method you may know from EMDR (Eye Movement Desensitisation and Reprocessing), a method used in post-traumatic stress disorder to release trauma memory. The client's legs start moving fast and faster. Then go ahead and help him to move his hands again, moving his head right and left suggesting nonverbally that he should do so more strongly.

v. Humming... ahn... ahn... ahn...

Or humming E, A, O.

E... E... E. Movement of the head or head passes concentrating on his forehead in the third eye area.

... A.. A... A. Deep touch at the heart region

and O.. O.. O.. at the solar plexus.

How do you know that your client is in Somnambulism?

i) The eyes are stark blinking, if you try to open them you will see only white color with rolling of eyes upward or they are looking at you with wider pupils as if he is staring at you.

ii)   The body becomes stiffer.

iii)   Contractions of the hands and feet.

iv)   The whole body curves around the spine like a bow.

v)   Rarely fits like epileptic fits, which is called a crisis.

vi)   There are some signs of this stage you cannot see, but you have to test on the client.

vii)   **Amnesia** – The client cannot think of a particular number or even his own name.

viii)   **Hallucination - positive or negative** – The client may see things that are not there in the room.

Positive Hallucination

Example: If you ask him to see a hanging picture of a sunset on the wall, which is not there, he will say yes he can see it and describe it to you.

Negative Hallucination

Example: You show him the pencil or pen and tell him he cannot see it, and he will tell you that he cannot see it.

Anesthesia

He cannot feel pain; you can use a needle to prick him or drop hot wax from a burning candle. He will not have any pain sensations. This property of Somnambulism is used by dental doctors and anesthetists to operate on minor surgeries.

Although these tests can be used in testing, here the client has to reply to your questions, and it is no longer part of nonverbal hypnosis.

Now we know we have reached the deep hypnotic state called Somnambulism. Only 30% of clients can go into this stage at the first hypnotic trance depending on their sensitivity, suggestibility, and polarity. In the second or third session, it is easier for him to relax and let go of his emotions out of his mind which he has been holding for many years, maybe from childhood or even from past lives. That is called - **Regression.**

Regression of Past Event

In pre-talk, if the hypnotist has a feeling that the client needs this, then in the Somnambulism stage, one can go ahead and produce the first regression by uttering the following questions to his unconscious mind:

- How old are you?

- Where are you?

- Are you alone or with somebody?

- Are you inside or outside? day or night etc.

To help to go into his past event even maybe in childhood. During the regression, the client may go into crisis.

Past Life Regression:

If you are planning to do a session on the past lives regression, then in pre-talk, you have to ask if he feels he remembers his past life events, some familiar images, places or déjà vu that he cannot explain.

Using Magnetic induction or Jellyfish induction as stated in the last chapter , you put your client down on the mattress holding the left hand of the client straight with your left hand to make it cataleptic. Same time your right hand moves his head as we have talked above 3-4 times left to right and then left and starts asking questions as in regression in past events but also the year and his name and name of the place where is located at that situation. He will start telling more about him and his life. At the end, he will tell you how he died.

Since it is no more nonverbal Hypnotherapy, I will not go into details. If you are interested, there are many books on past life regression. Sometimes the client has familiar problems to solve. He may have unfinished issues, conflicts with his father, mother, and siblings. This person may be dead and our client is still carrying this burden on him. He wants to work on it. Then you have to bring him with this person in his subconscious mind. That is called **Hypnodrama.**

How to bring him into this stage of Hypnodrama?

Same as above in pre-talk, you know his problem.

Method - The hypnotic induction with Magnetism, put the client on the floor, deepen him with head movements and long passes from head to toes. Then hold his both hands straight up and make them cataleptic and bring them together. You utter in his ears that his right hand is symbolic of himself and the left hand is the person with whom he has an issue to work with. Let him work on himself with his hands. Sometimes he may go into crisis if he has a problem reaching his solution.

In both stages of hypnotic trance - **Catalepsy and Somnambulism:**

The client's focus goes inward into his subconscious mind. We have seen how we have to recognise these stages nonverbally.

Now we want to know:

How to notice that our Client is working on his problem in his mind?

In deep trance, he will be moving his head and hands while handling his problem. He may feel coughing, crafting, vibrations of the body, and a change of breathing.

i) Coughing suggests he is refusing or distancing from his subconscious solution.

ii) Crafting the client means he has got the solution to his problem.

iii) Vibrations of the body and strong movement of the body suggest that he is releasing, discharging, letting go of his problem.

iv) The breathing changes from heavy, strong breathing to slow, calm breathing.

At the end of this stage, he may go to his imaginary **"Safe place"** where he feels fresh, peaceful, and joyful. One has to explain to him in the pre-talk that everybody has a safe place.

If he has a safe place to go in his mind to feel peaceful. For example, a sea face, sandy beach, hearing ocean waves, sitting at the bank of a river, walking in a garden or jungle, or even listening to his favorite music.

To bring him to that stage, you can use music 4-7 Hz.

At the end, he may go peacefully into deep sleep. That stage is called **Lethargy**. This is called **DELTA** waves state.

Sometimes he may go directly into the state, in which his all senses are in high alert but still he is in a deep joyful and blissful state. That is called the Ecstasy state.

ECSTASY: Somebody who used to do daily meditation for years can go into this stage. In this stage, electromagnetic waves are vibrating very strongly with 30-80 Hz in his brain, which is a **GAMMA** state.

Sadhus and Gurus, Monks, spiritual persons, who spend their lives in meditation and praying the whole day, may not have a problem going into Ecstasy. I have not talked about this stage yet. While only 1% of the clients can reach a blissful and Ecstasy state at the first hypnotic trance.

In the pre-talk, if the client tells you that he wants to experience self-confidence, peace, joy, or bliss in short for positive emotions.

The client may have negative emotions that he wants to get rid of and at the end wants to feel safe, strong, vital, blissful and alive.

In this case you have to work first on his negative emotions and then go on to perform Ecstasy.

In the first case, without any problem to work on, you go ahead with a Thumb holding induction then catalepsy. Once his hands are stiff, you can loosen them and bring them down and begin with performing the Ecstasy state.

Method

i) Make the client's head look upwards.

ii) Tap his forehead with your right index finger thinking that you are stimulating his third eye.

iii) Start doing passes from the face toward his crown from front and back. From right and left and moving hands up to his crown and upward as if you're connecting him with the Universe.

iv) At the same time, visualize yourself that he is going into the Ecstasy stage. Visualize with an image that he is entering Ecstasy and project it onto him and transmit to the Universe with strong willpower, the energy pushing by squeezing pelvic muscles. Wish him to go into a blissful state.

v) Make his both hands wide-open and start rotating clockwise by touching him.

vi) Soon he follows your hand and starts rotating himself. Then direct him to continue with it by guiding his hands.

vii) Start with humming E..E...E... or AUM...AUM. Music with 30-40 Hz.

viii) If the client is unable to rotate his hand, then hold his hands and put together his hands in the third eye chakra Mudra by forming a heart shape with touching his thumbs and middle fingers at the tip and his forefingers, ring fingers, and little fingers touching your forefingers. Let him hold hand in front of heart. As he goes deep into the Ecstasy stage, he may take his hands up in front of his forehead or even above the head.

How do you know that your client is in the Ecstasy state?

i) The client is hypersensitive to touch.

ii) Red eyes and nails.

iii) Eyes roll upward toward the crown of the head. When you try to open and see, you see only the white sclera of the eye.

iv) Looks like in a positive state of bliss with a smile on his face and red cheeks.

v) Starts singing or humming mantras or reacting to music and starts dancing.

In this stage, all his sense organs are hyperactive although he is in a trance. In this stage, he can go into his future or another world...another planet.

Third eye Chakra Mudra

Now we have learned how to induce our client into a hypnotic trance, how to keep him in trance with deepening stages - Catalepsy, Somnambulism, Hypnodrama, Crisis, Regression, and Ecstasy.

We can begin with Hypnotherapy. In the next chapter, we will learn about the treatment of physical and emotional pain, anxiety, negative emotions, and addictions.

> **Each crisis is beneficial. Each Crisis has an end. We try to transfer internal (mental) crisis to external (physical) Crisis.**
>
> **–Dr. Marco Paret**

8

Nonverbal Hypnotherapy

Nonverbal Hypnotherapy can be used for treating physical pain, emotional pain, past psychological trauma (PTSD), phobias, tinnitus, addictions like smoking, weight gain, etc., even in partner or family conflicts.

After the pre-talk with the client, you know what his problem is. Interestingly, the client does not have to talk during the therapy, and the Hypnotherapist is also silent. Often, he himself is in the trance and helps his client by imagining and projecting his ideas with strong willpower and electromagnetic energy.

Normally, I do 3 sessions with the client. At the first visit, you talk about Hypnosis and nonverbal hypnosis, how it works, so that he is at ease and not anxious about Hypnosis. You tell him that he will not do anything he does not want to do against his beliefs, morals, and will.

Then the client tells his personal problem in short, if he does not want to expose his privacy. If he wants to tell you in detail, that is okay too. Now you want to know the following:

Which, how, when, what, where questions.

1. How long he has had this problem, when was the first time he experienced the problem.

2. What emotions he has when he thinks about it.

3. Where does he feel it in his body?

Let him know that you will be giving him some nonverbal suggestions during the session. You will be gently touching and guiding him in the body movements you want him to perform. The session will be in silence in the room except you are humming or uttering some tones, or om mantra and sometimes music to make him relax.

It does help him to work on his problem. In the first session, you give him an experience of nonverbal Hypnosis and work on some elements of his problem. Normally, I give him an exercise, homework like Breathing, Awareness, or Energy exercise.

The second session is long, and the client has the possibility to work on this problem. In the third session, a short repetition of the second session, and in Post-talk, giving him information about self-hypnosis so that he knows how to deal with his problem in the future.

I have presented a case of a lady teacher in the introduction chapter where I used a light source from my mobile for hypnotic induction along with my magnetic gaze looking at her forehead, in between the eyebrows at the third eye. I could have used the Thumb holding method or any other methods you feel in your imagination to induce your client. Immediately you go ahead with those deepening methods we have discussed in the last chapter. Once you have your client in this stage and already thought of your therapy and project on him with your strong willpower and energy and let it go. Let it happen. Let the client's inner healer, his subconscious mind, take over.

Body Pain

We will talk about body pain treatment. Generally, body pain sessions are short and pain disappears like magic since we take attention away from his pain.

In body pain, you can use one of the quick induction methods and there is no need for long deepening of trance up to Somnambulism. You can treat your client in 3 short sessions.

Unless you notice that body pains are negative emotional pains of past psychological trauma. In that case, you need many sessions.

Headache

After hypnotic induction with point fixation in a sitting or standing position.

Method:

i) Stay on the right side of the client.

ii) Hold your right hand on the forehead and left hand at the back of the head at the occiput for 30 seconds and imagine that his mind is getting rebalanced and projecting this idea in him with your will and energy after deep inhalation during your slow exhalation through nose with pulling buttocks inward.

iii) Then your right hand touches his chest area near the heart and left hand on the forehead.

iv) Now with your right hand touching the solar plexus and left hand on the heart touching the heart.

Exercise at Home:

If the client's headache attack occurs at home. Show him how to rebalance his mind at home as follows:

i)   Focus on the light for 30 seconds. Then close his eyes.

ii) With closed eyes, he has to imagine the current passing from the right ear to the left ear. He has to do that for 5 times and now left ear to right ear for 5 times.

iii) Then the current passes from the occiput, back of the head through his third eye to the forehead. Again for 5 times and from front to back of the front for 5 times.

iv) Finally, open his eyes and look at the light again for 30 seconds. And close the eyes until the image of the light disappears from his inner eye-third eye.

Backache and Other Muscle and Joint Pain

In pre-talk, you have to ask your client to show the exact point of the pain. If it is unilateral or bilateral or central.

If the pain is recent or chronic over many years. When talking to him, you realize that he may have emotional pain, then you have to take in questioning his pain like treating a negative emotion. We call it psychosomatic pain.

In this case, the client needs deepening of the trance up to the Somnambulism stage, THETA wave state and may need Crisis, past event Regression as we have discussed in the last chapter.

For neuromuscular and joint pain, we need not have deep trance. You can use **Mesmeric passes** and strokes with stimulating hypnotic points for the hypnotic induction.

Once he is relaxed and in ALPHA Wave Trance State, you start with therapy.

Method:

i) Localize the point of pain. You can do some passes in the area. You can blow warm air at the point of pain.

ii) You stand behind the client and hold the right hand at the lower end of the spine coccyx bone and the other hand at the occiput, upper end of the spine.

iii) Now hold the hands facing palms on both sides of the spine at the level of the point of pain. If unilateral, ask his opposite side to help him with the weak side in your mind.

iv) If it is bilateral, rub your hands together and hold them open at the point of maximum pain.

v) Next, fold fingers together to make pointed hands with the intention that he will be pain-free and project his idea along with your energy through your hands. Now bring your hand to the solar plexus and massage and give him a sign that he has to see his pain in front of him at this level and work out for himself his pain. His pain will get digested and disappear. During this time, you stay in presence and keep looking at his nonverbal signs to see if he has successfully worked on his problem.

vi) At the end, rebalance his head by holding the right hand on the right side of the head and the left on the left side. Visualize that he is free from the pain and blow this idea on his head.

The same method can be used for neck pain, shoulder pain, sciatic pain, joint pains.

If you think his pain is emotional pain, then you have to know if he has a color or shape for his pain. If his pain is stationary or spinning, if so, clockwise or anticlockwise and does he want to get rid of it. What color and what type of shape he wishes for his pain. After therapy, tell him once he is in hypnotic trance, he should take the pain out of his body and hold it in front of him at the level of the solar plexus and imagine looking through the solar plexus to his pain in front of his navel outside the body. He should notice a change in color, shape and direction of spinning of his pain. If he feels good about it. He can bring the pain back into his body and feel relaxed. He may want to get rid of it by sending the pain away by making it bigger and bigger in black and white and see it at the horizon disappearing. In both cases, the Universe will take care of it.

Since we are working nonverbally, you tell him all this before the beginning of the hypnotic induction. Tell him you will guide him with nonverbal suggestions but you will not be talking.

Exercise at Home:

If a pain attack comes again, he should hold his hands over the pain area. He then takes a deep breath, holds it, and then slowly blows over the pain area. If he cannot reach the area, he should ask somebody to blow on his pain area.

If the pain is unilateral, next, holding one hand on the affected side and the other hand on the side which is healthy. He should think to himself that only this part of his body has pain and the other side is normal and healthy, even the rest of the whole body is healthy and strong and helping him to heal his pain. He knows that the pain is not in this part of the body but in his mind. He now knows that his soul is always happy, peaceful, joyful, and blissful. The soul wants to help his mind and body with loving care for overworked muscles, joints, or organs.

Di Pisa's Instant Healing Method:

It is a very fast fascination induction and pain therapy. An Italian Hypnotherapist, Di Pisa, used to heal 300 clients per day by this method every day. It took him 3-5 minutes for the Hypnotherapy per client. You can use this method for muscular pain, joint pains, and headache, even for chronic pain with negative emotions.

Method:

1. You put yourself in a positive emotion. Feel the energy in the body. Feel yourself strong, full of magnetic energy. You are a living Electromagnet. Ask the client where he

feels his pain and ask him to show you. Then you touch the pain area and feel the sensations.

2. Take his train of thought to something else. Make a joke so that he laughs and comes into a positive mood.

3. Look into the client's eyes with your strong, wide-open fascinated eyes to induce a fast hypnotic stage.

4. Imagine you have strong intention and willpower. You are going to heal him with strong fascination.

5. Keep the left hand on this pain area. After deep inhalation and during exhalation through the nose, project the idea or mental picture on him with a strong gaze.

6. Quickly bend forward and grab his head and neck from behind and move his head towards you and shake it.

7. Now stroke his shoulder down to his hands and wake him up.

8. Tell the client to test the pain. He will be surprised to see if it has gone. If it is reduced but not completely gone, do the procedure again. Generally, clients should have 3 sessions and exercises to do at home as we have discussed above.

Negative Emotions Healing:

After a pre-talk with the client, you know his problem. He should show where in the body he feels his emotions of the problem.

First, tell him to look at the light - point of fixation method for induction of Hypnotic Trance. He should think that the light is going in through the third eye to his mind. Then he should forget the problem and only feel the emotion. He has to bring that emotion to his solar plexus and work from there. He may feel warm and his emotion will get digested, burning like food gives you strong positive energy. With positive energy, you will wake up from the hypnotic trance.

Method:

Simple method using point fixation and achieving Catalepsy stage:

i) Hypnotic induction using light as point fixation for 30 seconds and relax. He now imagines that the light is going through his third eye to his mind. You stand in front of him gazing into his left eye and he should look into your right eye showing nonverbal communication with your right hand.

ii) Tell him not to blink, even if he blinks, no problem. When his eyes are feeling heavy, then he should close his eyes.

iii) When he closes his eyes or starts blinking and struggling to keep them open, then you massage both his eyelids and close his eyes with little pressure.

iv) You start doing long passes from head to toe and sides from head to hands.

v) Take his left hand and put it on his head and press it so he can hold it in place.

vi) Hold the right hand above the head and press at the arm, elbow, and hand to suggest to him to hold it there nonverbally. You may go ahead and make both his legs cataleptic in a similar manner.

vii) Now, your right hand on the solar plexus starts moving in a clockwise direction and your left hand on his forehead.

viii) You imagine that he is working on his problem at the solar plexus.

ix) Leave the client for some time with his hands and legs cataleptic.

x) You will notice that he has finished working on his emotions with his problem when he starts moving his hands.

xi) You can end the catalepsy and bring the hands slowly onto his lap and after a little shaking, put his legs on the ground.

xii) Then wake up the client by doing reverse passes from head to toe or blowing on his face.

Variation of Treatment Using NLP Technique

Localizing the emotion in the body. In pre-talk, ask about size, shape, color, stationary or spinning, if spinning clockwise or anticlockwise. Tell the patient once he is in the trance and brings his emotion into the solar plexus, he should bring it outside his body, look at it and notice, size and shape may change along with colors which he likes and try to spin it opposite to the original direction.

If changes that he likes and makes him feel happy, he should bring back to the body. If he feels becoming bigger and bigger and going far away in the horizon and disappearing into the universe. Once he is free from that emotion, he should go to his safe place. This you suggest in Pre-talk.

Negative Emotions of Past Event

If you think his negative emotion is in past event trauma, maybe in childhood or even in past lives. You feel the client may go into crisis or need regression in past events to change his emotion.

Method

During Pre-talk, you test his suggestibility by making him fall backward, sensitivity, and polarity. The client is easy to induce into hypnotic trance or may need a longer session. You tell the client you are putting a mat on the floor behind him, in case he falls down.

Standing position and using a point fixation in front of the Client and breathing. You stand on the right side of the client. Ask the client to go into that negative emotion.

    i)   Tell him to fix his gaze on the point, concentrate on the solar plexus, and breathe slowly.

ii)   You start matching his breathing, at the same time showing him with your hand to concentrate on the fix point, and concentrate on the solar plexus.

iii) You start stepping back and near to him slowly in all directions making noise of your shoes and humming… ahn…ahn…ahn…, keeping an eye on the Client. If he is sensitive, he may fall down.

iv)   When you come near the client, touch him randomly on different parts of the body - legs, arms, back, chest. Give extra pressure on his upper abdomen to remind him that he has to concentrate on the solar plexus and with hand directing the point of fixation for gazing.

v)   Now you change your breathing deep and strong and suggest that he do that by moving both his hands front and back.

vi)   At this time, you will see from his eyes that he is getting tired and blinking often and cannot keep them open. Now go quickly behind him, putting the left hand between his Axilla and hold him on your chest with the right hand closing his eyes and then slowly put him down on the floor. Keep holding his left hand with your left hand straight to make it cataleptic. At the same time, with your right hand moving his head side to side.

vii) See that his left hand stays straight, stiff, cataleptic. To test relaxation, hold his right leg above the ground and drop it down followed by the left leg. Bend both knees so that the feet are touching each other.

viii) Move the head from side to side again. Then touch his forehead and imagine that he is entering his first event. Bring his emotions into his legs and hands to rid them through strong movements with Willpower. Press your pelvic muscles during deep exhalation with an open mouth to project this idea, image towards his third eye using your strong magnetic energy.

ix) Press and tap hypnotic points on the chest at the sternum and move his legs, making them move, and say, "Release emotion in your mind"; you may whisper in his ears. Help him to enter the crisis. He will start moving his hands, legs, and whole body, sometimes curving his body over his spine.

x) After finishing the crisis, you can massage his solar plexus and start some relaxing music. The client may not experience a crisis and work silently. At the end, he will wake himself up or you can wake him up when you see he has finished and is struggling to wake up. He may go into Lethargy and sleep a little longer. With reverse passes from feet to head a few times or blowing on his face, one can wake him up if you feel he has worked on his emotions.

Variation of Treatment

These traditional ancient techniques can be used during our hypnotherapy if you are familiar with them or get interested in learning them. Since these techniques are nonverbal

I use them more often to stimulate energy points in the therapy.

1. **Chakra Cleansing:** You can perform chakra cleansing by releasing negative energy anticlockwise movements from root Chakra to crown Chakra and putting energy with clockwise direction on all 7 Chakras from crown Chakra with their colors. You can also produce energy by rubbing your both hands intensively and sprinkle it on all the Charas.

    Name of the Chakras and their colors

    Crown Chakra- Violet / white

    Third Eye Chakra- Indigo

    Throat Chakra- Light Blue

    Heart Chakra- Green / Pink

    Solar Plexus Chakra- Yellow

    Sacral Chakra- Orange

    Root Chakra- Red

    Chakra means "Wheel " and refers to energy points in our body in the ancient traditions of Hinduism and Buddhism denominated as Tantra.

2. **Acupressure Points:** You can also use acupressure points to stimulate relaxation and deepen trance in therapy by pressing them.

The Acupuncture Points

GB 20 (Gall bladder-Meridian 20) - This point is located behind the trapezius and sternocleidomastoid muscle at the lower border of the occiput. Useful for neck and back of the head, trigeminal neuralgia, facial paresis.

SJ 17 (Sanjiao-Meridian 17) – This point is below the earlobe, in the groove between the angle of the jaw and the mastoid. You can use it in the treatment of headache and dizziness.

Anmian Point: This point is on the head, about an inch from the soft depression immediately behind the earlobe towards the back of the head. It is a very important point for us to induce peaceful sleep. You can gently massage using your index fingers in circular movements on both sides of the client's neck at these points for relaxation, enhancing sleep, and pain reduction.

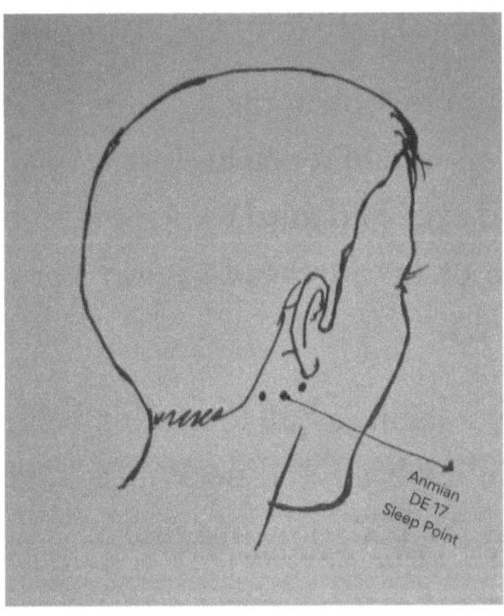

3. **Reiki Symbols:** Using various Reiki symbols on the heart and solar plexus. Reiki is an energy healing technique that uses life force energy to reduce stress and anxiety and encourage relaxation and deepens hypnotic trance.

Ball of Light Technique

This simple nonverbal technique can be used for clients with anxiety, fear, phobias, PTSD, and even tinnitus.

Method

1. Ask the client to sit comfortably on the chair and look at the light straight in front of him, about a meter away at the level of his head. The light should be of 70 watts and opal white in color. You can use light from your mobile in case you do not have any light.

2. Ask your client where he feels his emotion in the body. Ask him to recall the past event where he first felt that emotion. He can also think about the positive emotion he has with this event to feel.

3. Now ask him to look at the light for 30 seconds, then close his eyes. You should touch his forehead and tell him to look at the third eye. The third eye is said to be located around the middle of the forehead slightly above the junction of the eyebrows.

4. Ask him to imagine a ball formation behind the occiput (an area where his head and neck meet together). He should not look at the ball, only imagine it.

5. He should imagine that light continuously goes through his third eye and head and through the occiput into the ball.

6. The ball collects past events with his negative emotions and detaches from the body.

7. Ask him to imagine that the ball is going up and up, becoming smaller and smaller, and disappearing in the sky. Now tap his forehead and ask him to concentrate on his third eye. He should now think of his positive emotions.

8. Now he should open his eyes and once again look at the light for 30 seconds and close again until the shadow of the light from his mind goes away and think of positive emotions.

At the end, you can rebalance his head by holding both hands on the sides of his head.

Ball of light

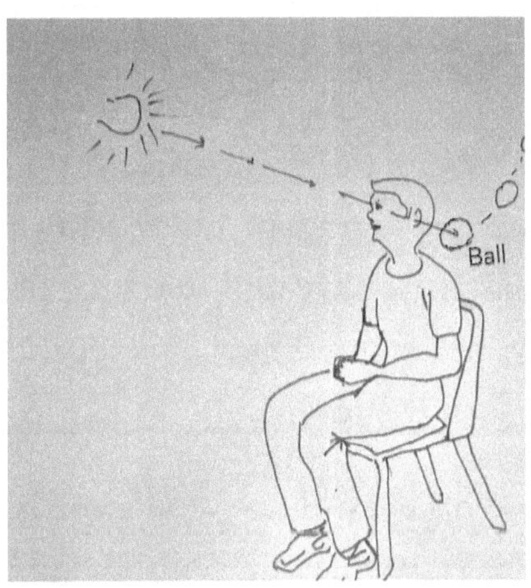

Magnetic Massage

The Magnetic Massage involves energetic, gentle touches on the body. Below is the complete method and its principles so that you can start using it with your clients from today onward.

Your client can lay down comfortably on the massage couch or relax in a chair. They should desire to receive the massage and relax with a clear mind, free from thoughts and emotions. They should enjoy it.

As it is a Magnetic Massage, it utilizes electromagnetic energy. First, visualize that you are healing your client and that they are enjoying it. This mental picture can be projected by squeezing your pelvic muscles during exhalation after deep inhalation on your client. The massage includes short and long passes, strokes, and gentle touches. This is the principle behind this therapy. It is relaxing and reduces physical and mental stress.

Now, let's move to the practical part of it. Explain to the client that it is not a massage like the usual physical massage, but an energetic massage that stimulates hypnogenic areas on the body. You are activating their inner healer.

Once everything is set and the client is in a sitting or lying position, bring the energy to the center of the forehead by first focusing your eyes with a magnetic gaze and touching the client's third eye region. Eventually, press between their eyebrows with your right thumb until the top of the forehead.

The client will close his eyes. If not, you close his eyes giving little pressure over his eyes with your both thumbs. Then you start performing long passes from head to toe. Followed by touching the top of the head-crown of the head and forehead at the same time with your right hand. Then hold his forehead with your right hand and back of the head with your left hand.

Next step is to stroke both eyelashes, eyelids and eyeballs. Slowly move the index finger of your right hand slowly over his nose with tender touch. then both cheeks and chin. Both earlobes give some more energy by putting powder in the ears-like action with your close right hand.

Now go to the back of your client and press both his shoulders downward with little pressure and then stroke arms downward till hands. Now, come again to the front of the client and start performing passes first from his right hand to the solar plexus, then his left hand to the solar plexus. Next, it passes from the right foot to the solar plexus and then from the left foot to the solar plexus. This is followed by clockwise rotatory movements of your right hand to stimulate the solar plexus. At this stage, one can perform additional rotatory passes at 4 corners of the stomach to include all energy points.

Now we are going to stimulate 7 chakras plus 2 more at the level of knees and at the level of feet by doing front and back passes at each chakra level. For that, you have to stay at the right side of the client and start from the top, Crown Chakra, by putting the right hand front on the top of the head and left hand behind. Next third eye chakra, followed by throat chakra, right hand in the front and left at back.

Followed by Heart chakra, Solar chakra, Sacral chakra and Root Chakra. We have 2 extra chakras for stimulation, one at the level of both knees and then ankles. Here, you can sprinkle more energy by rubbing hands with each other and generating energy to sprinkle all overall chakras. One can do this gesture 2 to 3 times to sprinkle all over the body.

You are giving Earth magnetic energy to your client by holding both ankles.

Lastly, to balance. Stay on the right side of the client and put your right hand on the Head and left hand on the Heart.

Holding for some time and wishing him love, stability and security in his life. Then, the right hand on the Heart and the left on the solar plexus, followed by both hands on the Solar plexus and visualize that your client has now been charged with full power, living energy, and living force with the help of Universal energy and Earth magnetic energy. Now his power bank is full.

Magnetic Massage

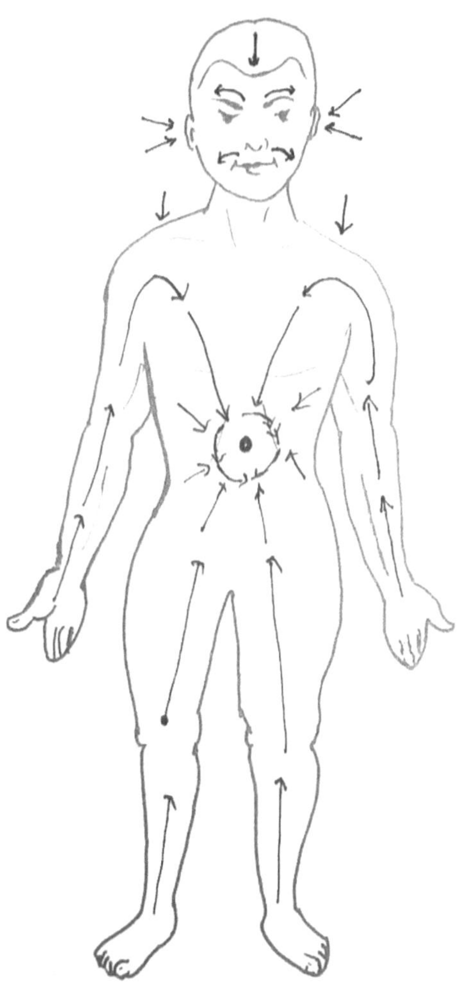

Addictions

Cigarette smoking, Alcohol, Drugs, Sugar,Gambling and Internet. Verbal hypnotherapy is time-consuming for both the hypnotherapist and the client. Nonverbal hypnotherapy, invented by Campanelli, is fast and lasts 4-5 minutes.

In the pre-talk, you have to inform the client that it is a very simple method and does not take a long time. It has been used by many well-known celebrities. We do not know exactly how it works, but it has been successful in 75% of smokers who want to stop smoking.

Then, ask some personal questions - how long has he been smoking, since when did he start smoking, and does he want to quit today? Then, he has to throw away all his cigarettes, breaking them into small pieces and showing him the dustbin.

Once he has gotten rid of all cigarettes, proceed to the next step.

Method

The client is in a sitting position. You stand behind the client and do some passes for the induction of Hypnotic Trance.

i) Press the occiput (back of the head) with your left hand and the third eye (forehead) in the front. Then, rotate his head with your hands side to side and hold his head between your hands.

ii) Imagine and produce the mental image that he is stopping cigarettes now.

iii) With strong intention and willpower, blow the idea that he stops smoking on his crown of the head by pressing your pelvic muscles and exhaling long after deep inhalation with the mouth slightly open.

iv) Now come to the front of the client and touch his forehead with your left hand and his heart with your right hand. Stroke his arms down till his hands as if pushing him back. Do this forehead and heart touching 3 times.

v) Then, place your left hand on his forehead and your right hand at the solar plexus. Perform passes from arms to legs.

vi) Hold both his legs at the ankles to keep his feet on the floor to discharge the bad energy onto the Earth, followed by passes on the whole spine from the neck up to the sacrum.

vii) Wake him up.

viii) Tell him that he should not drink coffee and alcohol for the next 48 hours. This is a very easy method with a 75% success rate that one can try.

You can use this method for other Addictions too.

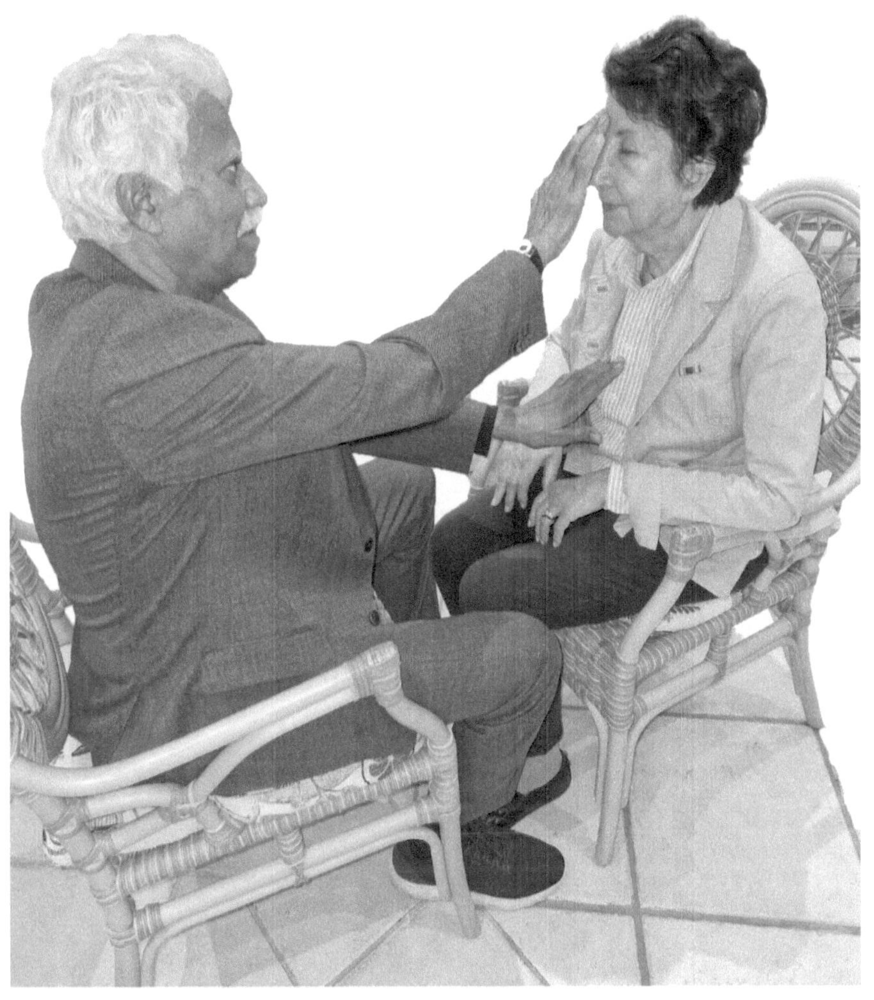

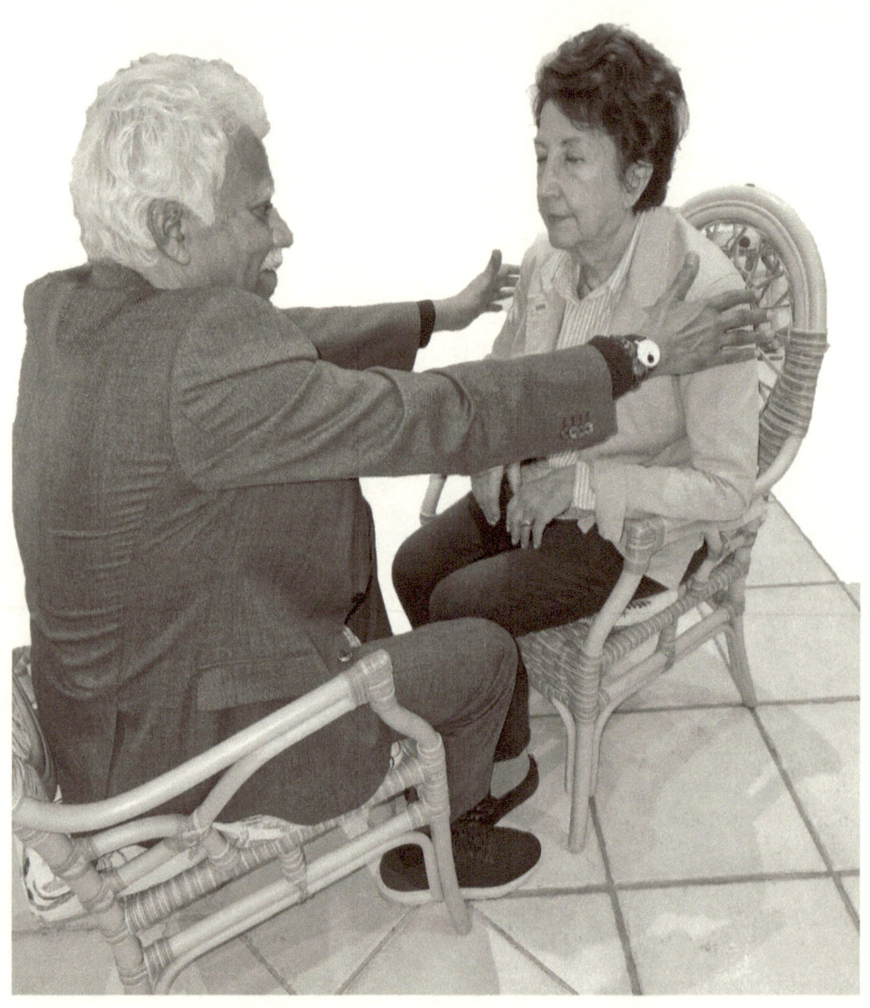

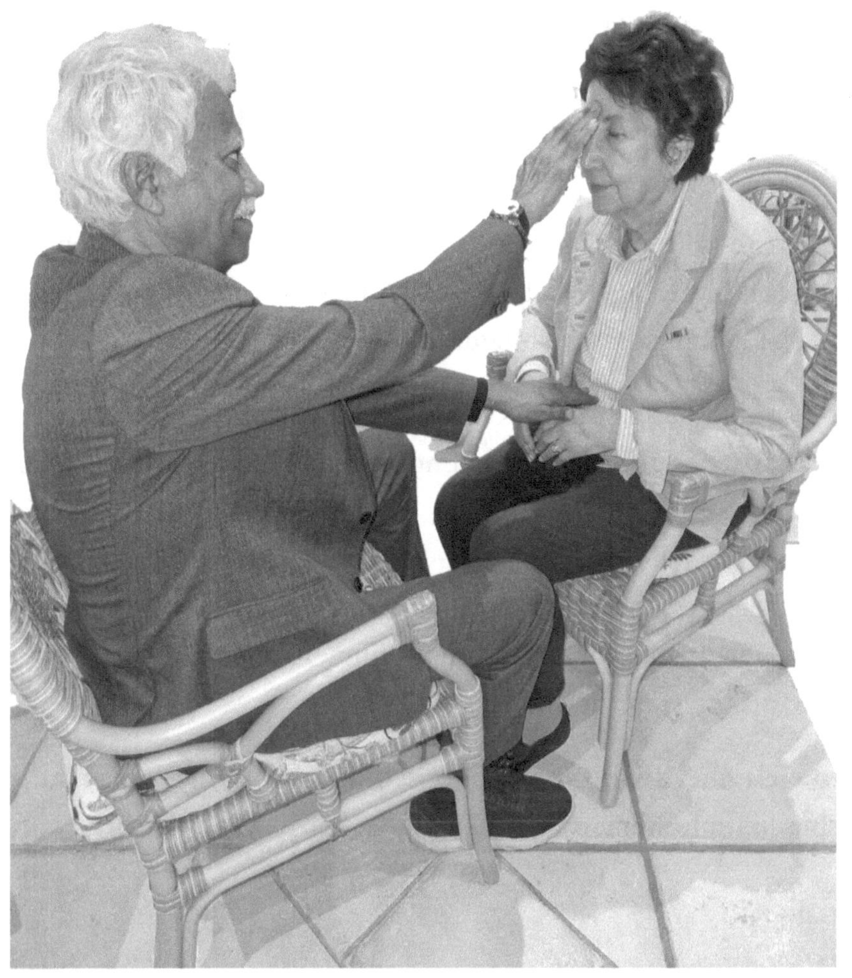

Weight Loss

Since with weight loss problems, many women come to the hypnotherapist. As a gynecologist, I have treated only women with weight loss and body image problems.

I hope you do not take me as gender biased. Until now, I have used the male client in my presentations.

We assume here our client is a lady and wants to reduce weight and have her slim figure again. Is it possible? Yes, it is possible with nonverbal Hypnosis and dealing with all her systems in the body.

In the Pre-talk, you can ask her about her problem. How long has she been suffering? Does she remember her ideal figure? If not, can she imagine her wish figure?

You should prepare a glass of water, if possible, crystal glass. Tell her that when she is in the hypnotic trance, with closed eyes, she should imagine her ideal figure after her weight loss, which she desires once she has his image in front of her eyes. She should open her eyes, look into the glass, and see her new figure inside the water. It may be a picture or film. It does not matter, then drink all the water in the glass.

Now go ahead with the hypnotic induction using point fixation using light, holding a light just above her head.

Method

i.   Close her eyes.

ii.   Give her the glass of water and show her to look in the water. She has to see her own new figure inside the water. Once she is satisfied then she should drink the water.

iii.   Stop imagining- she should not think any more.

iv.   Then, you do head movements from right to left.

v. Followed by long passes head to foot front, back, and sides.

vi. **Endocrine glands** – to stimulate Endocrine glands -Pineal gland, Pituitary gland, Thyroid gland, Pancreas and Genital organs.

Begin by touching her forehead for the pineal gland and pituitary glands. Left hand on the forehead and right hand on neck, the thyroid area, next keeping left hand on the forehead and right hand on the upper part of the stomach, left side- pancreas area and lower abdomen in Genital area.

vii. **Nervous system**- you perform 9 passes at the level of Chakras plus at the level knees and feet Crown Chakra- holding both hands on the top of the head, then left hand behind the head and right hand on the forehead, at the third eye chakra. Next, at the level of the throat, followed by heart chakra, right hand in front of the client and left hand behind the client at the level of heart, then solar plexus chakra at the level of the upper abdomen, Sacral chakra- lower abdomen, then the level of knees and at the end holding both ankles for some time.

viii. **Psychology** –Emotions- putting left hand on the forehead right hand on the heart, forehead to solar plexus and last left hand on the heart and right hand on solar plexus.

ix. **Magnetic Energy**- touching forehead and solar plexus 3 times.

x.   **Balancing polarities** by holding the right and left wrist.

xi. **Re-balancing the mind**-right hand on the head and left hand on the solar plexus.

xii. This whole procedure you can repeat 3 times at the same session or 3 consecutive sessions.

Once therapy is finished, you can wake her up and give her exercise to do at home daily.

Exercise to Do at Home

Before starting breakfast, lunch, and dinner, she should have a glass of water. See her ideal figure in it, concentrate on it, and drink the water.

We have now seen some nonverbal Hypnotherapy possibilities. We will go on to learn Self-hypnosis in the next and final chapter of this practical book.

9

Miscellaneous

Self-Hypnosis:

How does it work? You may ask yourself.

There is no need for help from the hypnotist. You do yourself like a meditation. The difference is only that you want to work on your problem and ask for your subconscious mind to help you. Your subconscious mind wants only best things for you. For example, if you want to reduce weight, then you have to think and talk about healthy food and its benefits. If you keep saying, I have to stop eating ice cream, chocolate or cake again and again, then you see them everywhere and buy and eat ice cream and chocolate cake.

If you want your subconscious mind to work on your problem. You have to think, feel, behave and talk only about what you want and not what you do not want. Talk positive all the time about what you want to eat to reduce your weight. The subconscious mind is like a machine. It works day and night to keep us healthy, peaceful, and joyful in the body and mind, as well as to keep us alive. It works every second, minute, and whole day, year after year, from birth to the end, through breathing, blood circulation, and digestion, and it wants us to stay safe and sound. It gives us solutions through our life experiences stored as a vast memory bank. You can trust your subconscious mind.

Now, I will show you how to get in contact with it through the critical factors. Once you are in the subconscious mind, it will go through your problem with the help of old events and memories, guide you on the right track, and show you possibilities for solving your problem. It may not be immediately, but in the next 3-4 weeks, you start to get results. You will have a WOW effect. You have to thank your subconscious mind first.

Method

You sit comfortably and feel the feet on the floor, feel the chair in which you are sitting. Be in presence. Empty your mind. Then concentrate on a fixed point in front of you or a light or a candle will do. Gazing at it eventually your eyes are going to get tired then close them. You have just done the hypnotic Induction on yourself.

Another easy method is to look up at the crown of your head with closed eyes. In a few seconds, you will feel drowsy. Begin with the awareness exercise, which we have discussed in chapter 4.

Deep breathing and concentrating on the body parts: toes, feet, legs, hips, abdomen, back, chest and head. Your concentration and awareness should be in your body, and relax; let go of yourself. When you have finished organ scanning, go to your inner-world solar plexus. Think that The solar plexus is your Enteric evolutionary brain and see from there.

Start thinking about your problem. Feel the emotion that arises with the problem at the solar plexus. If you feel the emotion in another part of the body, for example, in the heart, then first go to the heart and feel the emotion and then bring that emotion to the solar plexus. Then, forget the problem and concentrate only on the emotion, their color and their shape and size.. Feel free to change the color,shape and size you want. If you find the change in the emotion in a positive way and you feel well about it, then slowly go into your safe place, your own imaginary place where you feel peace, joy and bliss. About your safe place, I have already talked about in chapter 7.

It may be at the sea on a sandy beach or in the mountains, in the garden, on the river bank, even in the jungle where you feel well, peaceful and you get good feelings and positive emotions and stay there.

Suppose you do not find a change in the shape or color of your emotions. Then visualize the emotion with its color and shape outside your body in front of your navel and make it black and white in color. Make it bigger and bigger going far away, like on the screen at the drive-in theater. Then go ahead and make it still bigger and bigger at the end of the horizon and disappear. Then you go into your imaginary safe place and stay there as long as you want. Slowly, you come back into your present state by opening your eyes with a smile.

This hypnotherapy method can also be used on your client.

Clairvoyance:

Clairvoyance is a French word which means "Hellseher ability." The direct English translation is "clear" or "bright vision." It means the power to see the future or to see the things that other people cannot see. Some people have the perception to see in time and space, they can see your past, past life experiences, in the future what is going to happen in your life next, even now in the present moment. They have developed sensations in the sensory, physical perception, like they have a sixth sense. The sixth sense means to see through the third eye or spiritual eye. This phenomenon is more studied in Parapsychology. It is not a magical or supernatural power. Although some people are naturally talented, one has to have sensory feelings. Mindfulness, presence, and spiritual intuition to develop clairvoyance.

How to develop Clairvoyance?

All the ancient cultures knew about it through meditation, Siddhi (liberation), shamanism even today practiced in many religions.

You have to develop paranormal skills and become a psychic person.

i)   Daily Meditation

ii) Visualization

iii) To write a Dream book.

iv) During the Hypnosis to achieve an Ecstasy stage.

You have to train daily. Once you get the results you will be curious and will experiment with it more often.

Method

You stand in front of a mirror. The light source is behind you, projecting onto the mirror. You observe the reflection of light in the mirror. Think about your friend or relative and consider where he or she might be, then stay passively in their presence. Send it to the Universe; it will take care of it and wait for the results. As I said before, practice... practice. Practice makes you a master. Once you're a master, your subconscious mind takes over your job. You are like a medium between the Universe, Earth, and your client.

Telepathy

Telepathy is the ability to read somebody's mind or communicate with someone mentally without using words or other physical signals. Here, both minds work together. Before the time of the telegraph and telephone, people often used this method to communicate with each other over long distances, perhaps thousands of kilometers apart.

i) **Mental Reading:** Thought-reading skills involve detecting using Ideomotor movements and psychic ability. In mental reading, only the operator is involved; the receiver is passive. Mental reading can involve past events, the future, or the present.

ii) **Emotional Telepathy:**

Here, emotional transfer occurs between 2 people through tactile sensations.

This involves accessing collective wisdom.

iii) **Mental Suggestions:** In this, thoughts are transferred from the hypnotist to the client.

Method

You have an intention to perform a hypnotic trance on your client. Imagine what you want to do. Make a mental image or a film in front of your eyes. Now, with your intention and Willpower, using strong energy, you have to project the mental image of your client. After a deep inhalation, you squeeze your pelvic muscles, and with magnetic eyes and magnetic hands in front of his magnetic breathing, project the image in his forehead between his eyebrows, this third eye, and think strongly that he will get it. At the same time, you can also send it to the Universe.

During hypnotic induction and hypnotherapy, if you use this method for mental suggestion, you will have more success and excellent results.

10

The END

I have not yet told you the secret of nonverbal Hypnosis. Dr Anton Mesmer knew and many nonverbal Hypnotists know. You observe your client. He wants to work on his problem. You want to get rid of his problem. His subconscious mind also wants him to be well, peaceful, joyful and healthy.

He will go into hypnosis himself. Every hypnosis is a Self-hypnosis.

You do not have to do much .Do not get worried and stressed. Just stay in the presence.

He will work on his problem himself. Sometimes he may stay long in a cataleptic position or in crisis may get hurt by violent cramps. You make sure that he is not getting hurt .

I cannot end this book without telling you how to bring your client back to a full awake state with no words. Bringing it back to normal is called Dehypnosis.

Dehypnosis:

The client works on his emotional problem for 20-25 minutes and then usually goes into his "safe place"-in a bliss state and stays there another 15 minutes. From Pre-talk to the End of the hypnotherapy takes about an hour. The client starts moving slowly on his hands, legs, and positions. Sometimes he comes back to normal by opening his eyes.

You observe his movements and feel that he wants to come back, and then you stand behind him, hold his hands on both sides of his head, and try to make mental suggestions.

You make a mental picture that he is opening his eyes and smiling at you. You have to develop this skill. You can also directly go for reverse passes from the feet to the head a few times. If he is still in deep trance, then you can blow on his face or give him small touches on his left cheek. 95% of Clients open their eyes and smile on their faces, happy to see you again after a trance.

The last 5 % may need verbal suggestions to come to a normal state.

In that case you whisper in his ear to wake up. You may leave the client in his position and not wake him. Perhaps he likes that. They will not take more than 2 hours. If he feels thirsty or wants to go to the toilet he will wake up.

Hypnotic sleep is a concentrated sleep, so 15-minute hypnotic sleep is like 3 hours of deep sleep. Just before Dehypnosis, we should give our client.

Post-hypnotic Suggestions:

Post-hypnotic suggestions are about his well-being, confidence, health, success,happiness etc.In nonverbal Hypnotherapy, you can give mental suggestions projecting on him. One can use verbal suggestions whispering in his ear or even you can tell him that you are counting 3-2-1 and by count one he should open his eyes with a smile on his face.

When we are talking about verbal suggestions. Modern hypnosis is 100% verbal Hypnosis. Many new generation hypnotists, after experiencing how easy it is to work with nonverbal Hypnosis using Mesmerism, Magnetism, Fascination etc. More and more Hypnotists now use a combination of both nonverbal and verbal methods.

I call it combo-hypnosis.

Hope you will start with nonverbal Hypnosis with great enthusiasm. I wish you all the success.

OM